Caroline C. Leighton

# Life at Puget Sound

With Sketches of Travel in Washington Territory, British Columbia, Oregon, and California, 1865-1881

Caroline C. Leighton

**Life at Puget Sound**
*With Sketches of Travel in Washington Territory, British Columbia, Oregon, and California, 1865-1881*

ISBN/EAN: 9783337205904

Printed in Europe, USA, Canada, Australia, Japan

Cover: Foto ©Andreas Hilbeck / pixelio.de

More available books at **www.hansebooks.com**

# LIFE AT PUGET SOUND

WITH

## SKETCHES OF TRAVEL

IN

WASHINGTON TERRITORY, BRITISH COLUMBIA, OREGON, AND CALIFORNIA

1865–1881

BY

CAROLINE C. LEIGHTON

BOSTON
LEE AND SHEPARD, PUBLISHERS
NEW YORK
CHARLES T. DILLINGHAM
1884

# PREFACE.

THE following selections from observations and experiences during a residence of sixteen years on the Pacific Coast, while they do not claim to describe fully that portion of the country, nor to give any account of its great natural wealth and resources, yet indicate something of its characteristic features and attractions, more especially those of the Puget Sound region.

This remote corner of our territory, hitherto almost unknown to the country at large, is rapidly coming into prominence, and is .now made easy of access by the completion of the Northern Pacific Railroad. The vast inland sea, popularly known as Puget Sound, ramifying in various directions, the wide-spreading and majestic forests, the ranges of snow-capped mountains on either side, the mild and equable climate, and the diversified resources of this favored region, excite the astonishment and admiration of all beholders. To the lovers of the grand and beautiful, unmarred as yet by any human interference, who appreciate the freedom from conventionalities which pertain to longer-settled portions of the globe, it presents an endless field for observation and enjoyment. There is already a steady stream of emigration to this new "land of promise," and every thing seems to indicate for it a vigorous growth and development, and a brilliant and substantial future.

# CONTENTS.

## CHAPTER I.



## CHAPTER II.



## CHAPTER III.

## CHAPTER VIII.



## CHAPTER IX.



## CHAPTER X.



## CHAPTER XI.

## CHAPTER XII.



## CHAPTER XIII.



## CHAPTER XIV.

## CHAPTER XV.

# LIFE AT PUGET SOUND.

## I.

**At Sea. — Mariguana Island. — Sea-Birds. — Shipwreck. — Life on Roncador Reef. — The Rescue. — Isthmus of Panama. — Voyage to San Francisco. — The New Baby.**

**ATLANTIC OCEAN, May 26, 1865.**

IT is a great experience to feel the loneliness of the sea, — to see the whole circle of the heavens, and nothing under it but the rising and falling water, from morning till night, day after day.

The first night we were out the porpoises came up at twilight, and sported round the vessel. I saw some sea-birds that seemed to be playing, — running and sliding on the green, glassy waves. In the wake of the vessel were most beautiful changing colors. Little Nelly S. sat with us to watch the phosphorescence. She said, "The stars in the sea call to me, with little fine voices, 'Nelly, Nelly, are you alive?'"

May 27, 1865.

We have had our first sight of land, — Mariguana, a coral island, one of the Bahamas. Every one stood in silence to see it, it was so beautiful. The spray dashed so high, that, as it fell, we at first took it for streams and cascades. It was just at sunrise; and we cast longing looks at the soft green hills, bathed in light. Now it is gone, and we have only the wide ocean again. But a new color has appeared in the water, — a purplish pink, which looks very tropical; and there are blotches of yellow seaweed. Some of it caught in the wheel, and stopped it. The sailors drew it up, and gave it to the children to taste. It was like a little fruit, and they say the birds eat it.

The sea is growing quite rough. I was thinking of being a little afraid, the vessel plunged so; but Mother Cary's chickens came out, and I thought I might as well consider myself as one of them, and not in any more danger than they are.

Caribbean Sea, May 28, 1865.

We have had a great experience of really rough weather. The spray dashed over the deck, and only the hardiest could keep up. Any one who tried to move was thrown off his feet. Preparations were made for divine service by lashing two boxes together in the middle of the deck, and spreading a flag over them. It was conducted by a Scotch Presbyterian minister. As he began his prayer, he received quite an addition to his congregation, in a flock of great birds, that appeared on my side of the vessel. They wheeled round, and settled down softly together. I do not know what they are, but suppose they are gulls of some kind. They have long, narrow wings, brown, with a little black, and snow-white underneath. I am half inclined to envy these wild, soulless creatures, that know no fear.

RONCADOR REEF, June 5, 1865.

On Tuesday morning, May 30, between three and four o'clock, we were awakened by the sharp stroke of the engine-bell, a deep grinding sound, and the sudden stopping of the vessel. We knew that we had not arrived at our port of destination, and felt instinctively that something extraordinary had happened. For a moment all was silence; then inquiries arose from all sides, as to what was the matter. The engine seemed to be in a great state of commotion: and the vessel began to writhe with a heavy, laborious movement, as if attempting to free herself from the grasp of some monster. We dressed hastily, and went into the cabin, where we found a good many of the passengers, and learned that the vessel had struck on a coral-reef. We put on life-preservers, and sat waiting until daylight, expecting every moment the vessel would split. As soon as it was light enough, we went upon deck, and saw the sailors cut away the masts and smoke-stacks, which went over the side of the ship. The water dashed over the deck, so that we were obliged to go below. It seemed there as if we were under the ocean, with the water breaking over our heads. Chandeliers, glasses, and other movable articles were crashing together around us. The cabin was filled with people, quietly sitting, ready for they knew not what. But among all the seven hundred passengers there was no shrieking nor crying nor groaning, except from the little children, who were disturbed by the noise and discomfort. How well they met the expectation of death! Faces that I had passed as most ordinary, fascinated me by their quiet, firm mouths, and eyes so beautiful, I knew it must be the soul I saw looking through them. Some parties of Swedish emigrants took out their little prayer-books, and sat clasping each other's hands, and reading them. A missionary bound for Micronesia handed out his tracts in all directions, but no one took much notice of them. Generally, each one seemed to feel that he could meet death alone, and in his own way.

In the afternoon a faint semblance of land was seen off on the horizon, and a boat was sent out to explore. It was gone a long time, and as night approached was anxiously looked for. Just about dark, it appeared in sight. As it drew near, we saw the men in it waving their hats, and heard them shouting, by which we knew they had succeeded in finding land. The men on the vessel gave a hearty response, but the women could not keep back their tears.

That night the women and children were lowered with ropes, over the side of the vessel, into boats, and taken to a raft near by, hastily constructed on the rocks at the surface of the water, from loose spars, stateroom-doors, and such other available material as could be secured from the vessel. All night long we lay there, watching the dim outline of the ship, which still had the men on board, as she rose and fell with each wave, — the engine-bell tolling with every shock. The lights that hung from the side of the vessel increased the wild, funereal appearance of every thing about us. They continually advanced and receded, and seemed to motion us to follow them. There was a strange fascination about them, which I could not resist; and I watched them through the whole night.

At daylight the next morning the ship's boats began to take us over to the island discovered the day before, which was slightly elevated above the surface of the water, and about four miles distant from the wreck. As we approached the shore, some new birds, unlike any I had seen before, — indolent-looking, quiet, and amiable, — flew out, and hovered over the boat, peering down at us, as if inquiring what strange creatures were about to invade their home. Probably they had never seen any human beings before. The sailors said they were "boobies;" and they certainly appeared very unsophisticated, and quite devoid of the wit and sprightliness of most birds.

Only a few persons could be landed at a time, and I wandered about at first almost alone. It was two days before all the passengers were transferred. Every thing was so new and strange, that I felt as if I had been carried off to another planet; and it certainly was a great experience, to walk over a portion of the globe just as it was made, and wholly unaltered by man.

I thought of an account of a wreck on this

same water I had once read, in which the Caribbean was spoken of as the most beautiful though most treacherous of seas, and the intensity of color was mentioned. Such rose-color I never saw before as in the shells and mosses we find here, nor such lovely pale and green tints as the water all about us shows.

We have been here on this bare reef six days, with the breakers all around us, and do not know whether we shall get off or not. We amuse ourselves every morning with looking at the pert little birds, as queer as the boobies, though quite different from them, that sit and nod to each other incessantly, and give each other little hits with their bills, as if these were their morning salutations, — a rough way of asking after each other's health.

San Francisco, July 2, 1865.

We are safely here at last, after forty-two days' passage, — longer than the children of Israel were in the wilderness. When we return it will be by a wagon-train, if the Pacific Railroad is not done.

When we landed on Roncador Reef, we had no data for conjecturing where we were, except that we remembered passing the island of Jamaica at twilight on the evening preceding the wreck. We were afterwards informed that the vessel was seized by a strong current, and borne far away from her proper course. How gay we were that night, with our music and dancing, exhilarated all the more by the swiftness of the white, rushing water that drove us on to our fate!

The heat on the island was so intense, that our greatest necessity was for some shelter from the sun. The only materials which the place furnished us were rocks of coral, with which we built up walls, over which were spread pieces of sail from the vessel. We lived in these lodges, in little companies. We sat together in ours in the daytime, and could not leave our shelter for a moment without feeling as if we were sunstruck. Every night we abandoned it, and slept out on the rocks; but the frequent little showers proved so uncomfortable that we were driven to great extremity to devise some covering. R.'s ingenuity proved equal to the emergency. He secured an opportunity to visit the vessel (which held together for some days) in one of the boats which were continually plying between her and the island, bringing over all available stores. All the mattresses and other bedding that could be secured had been distributed, mostly to the mothers and children.

His penetrating eye detected the materials for a coverlet in the strips of painted canvas nailed to the deck. He managed without tools to tear off some pieces, and, by untwisting some tarred rope, to fasten them together; thus providing a quilt, which, if not comfortable, was at least waterproof, and served to draw over us when a shower came on. It was no protection, however, against the crabs, large and small, that used to crawl under it, and eat pieces out of our clothes, and even our boots, while we were asleep. These crabs were of the *hermit* order. Each one, from the minutest to the largest, had taken possession of the empty shell of some other creature, exactly large enough for him, and walked about with it on his back, and drew himself snugly into it when molested. Every little crevice in the rocks had a white or speckled egg in it when we landed, and from these we made a few good meals. The one day the women spent on the island alone with the birds passed in the most friendly manner; but after the men and boys came, the larger ones abandoned us.

We felt sorry not to bring away some of the beautiful shells which were plentiful there, and more gorgeous than any thing I ever saw before. While the living creature is in them, they are much brighter than after it is dead; and in the length of time it takes to bring them from tropical countries, they fade almost like flowers. Mrs. S. was so enterprising, and, I must say, so unæsthetic, as to try to concoct a meal from the occupants of some of the large conch-shells taken from the beach, cooking it for a considerable length of time in a large brass kettle, the only available utensil. Those who partook of it in our little group had cause to repent of their rashness; but we did not like to charge the injury to the lovely creatures which were sacrificed for this feast, preferring to "blame it on" to the brass kettle, as the California children would express it. The more cautious ones contented themselves with their two sea-biscuits and fragment of beef or pork per day, which were the regular rations served to each from the stores saved from the ship. Some surface water, found among the rocks, was carefully guarded, and sparingly dealt out.

After we had been four or five days on the island, two of the ship's boats were sent out to seek assistance, manned by volunteer crews; one headed for Aspinwall, which was thought to be about two hundred and fifty miles distant, and the other to search for what was supposed to be the nearest land.

Very early on the morning of the tenth day we heard the cry of "A sail!" We started up from our rocky beds, and stood, without daring to speak. There was a little upright shadow, about as large as a finger, against the sky. Every eye was turned to it, but no one yet dared to confirm it; and, even if it were a sail, those on board the vessel might not see our island, it was so low, or our flag of distress, as we had nothing on which to raise it very high. We stood for several minutes, without daring to look at each other with the consciousness that we were saved. We presently saw that there were two little schooners beating up against the wind, directly towards us, and that they carried the red English flag. They had been catching turtles on the Mosquito Coast. As soon as our boat reached them, they unloaded their turtles (which occupied them a day), with the exception of three large ones which they reserved for us, and then started at once.

These small vessels were unequal to carrying away half the people on the island, and they had no arrangements for the comfort of passengers. A considerable number decided to embark on them, and commenced doing so; while the larger part of the company remained on the spot, to take their chance of escape in some other way, since communication with the world was now established.

The next day we were all rejoiced by the appearance of two United-States gunboats from Aspinwall, which point was reached by our other boat, after a rough experience; the waves having capsized her during the passage, and swallowed up the provisions and nautical instruments.

It was then decided that all the company should be taken to Aspinwall by the United-States vessels, and their boats and ours were at once put to service in transferring the people from the island; who, as they gathered up such fragments of their property as had been rescued from the wreck, and tied it up in bedquilts or blankets, shouldered their bundles, and moved slowly down to the point of departure, — their garments weather-stained and crab-eaten, some of them without shoes or hats, and all with much-bronzed faces, — presented a picturesque and beggarly appearance, in striking contrast to their aspect before the wreck.

We were treated with the greatest kindness by every one connected with the gunboats. They took us in their arms, and carried us into the boats, and stood all night beside us, offering ice-water and wine. They greatly bewailed our misfortunes, and told us, that, when they heard of our condition, they put on every pound of steam the vessels would bear, in order to reach us as speedily as possible, fearing that some greater calamity might befall us, — that our supply of water might entirely fail, or that the trade-wind might change, and a storm bring the sea over the island. They told us, too, that we were very far off the track of vessels; and, if our boats had failed to bring succor, in all probability no one would ever have come there in search of us.

The two schooners decided to remain a while, and wreck the vessel. As we steamed away from the reef, we passed her huge skeleton upon the rocks, the bell still hanging to the iron part of the frame.

On the second day we reached Aspinwall, and disembarked. As we sat on the wharf, in little groups, on pieces of lumber or on our bundles, waiting for arrangements to be made for our transportation across the Isthmus, a black man, employed there, fixed his eye upon our dark-skinned Julia, and, approaching, asked if she "got free in the Linkum war." I told him that she did, and asked him where he came from. He said he was from Jamaica; and I said, "I suppose you have been free a long time?" to which he replied, with great energy, "Before I was born, I was free," and repeated it again and again, — "before I was born."

We found that Julia, to whom all things were new in the land of freedom, thought that the island where we spent so many days was a regular stopping-place on the way to California, and that the wreck was a legitimate mode of stopping; as one day she inquired if that was the way they always went to San Francisco, and said, if she had known travelling was so hard, she would not have started. This accounted for her equanimity, which surprised me, after the vessel struck the reef, as she sat quietly eating her cakes, while every thing was going to destruction around us, and the sea broke above our heads.

In crossing the Isthmus of Panama, we were delighted with the neat appearance of the natives, whom we saw along the roadside, or sitting in their little huts near by, which were made of the trunks of the tall palm-trees, in columns, open at the side, and thatched with leaves. These people were clad in clean white garments, the women with muslins and laces drooping from their bare shoulders, and with bright flowers in their hair.

On reaching Panama, the women there greeted

us with great kindness and sympathy. One of them threw her arms around one of the first women of our party that she saw, and exclaimed, "Oh, we have thought so much about you! we were afraid you would die for want of water." It seemed strange that they should have cared so much, when a little while before they never knew of our existence. I felt as if I had hardly had a chance before in my life to know what mere humanity meant, apart from individual interest, and how strong a feeling it is. We realized still more the kindness of these "dear, dark-eyed sisters," when we opened the trunk of clothing which they sent on board the "America," the steamer that took us to San Francisco.

The voyage up the Pacific coast was long and wearisome. For some days we felt seriously the ill effects of the island life and the tropic heat, and could only endure; until, one morning, we came up on deck, and there were the beautiful serrated hills of Old California. We had rounded Cape St. Lucas, and had a strong, exhilarating breeze from the coast, and began to be ourselves again.

The monotony of our sea-life was broken by one event of special interest,—the addition of another human being to our large number. I must mention first,—for it seems as if they brought her,—that all one day we sailed in a cloud of beautiful gray-and-white gulls, flying incessantly over and around us, with their pretty orange bills and fringed wings and white fan-tails. They were very gentle and dove-like. They staid with us only that day. The last thing that I saw at night, far into the dark, was one flying after us; and, the next morning, we heard of the birth of the baby. She was christened in the cabin, the day after, by the Micronesian missionary, in the presence of a large company. A conch-shell from the reef served as the christening-basin. The American flag was festooned overhead; and, as far as possible, the cabin was put into festive array. She was named "Roncadora America," from the reef, and the vessel on which she was born. The captain gave her some little garments he was carrying home to his own unborn baby, and the gold ties for her sleeves. When her name was pronounced, the ship's gun was fired; then the captain addressed the father, who held her, and presented him with a purse of fifty dollars from the passengers, ending in triumph with—

"And now, my friends, see Roncadora,
With freedom's banner floating o'er her."

The father then uncovered her; she having made herself quite apparent before by wrestling with her little fists under the counterpane, and uttering a variety of wild and incomprehensible sounds. She proved a handsome baby, large and red, with a profusion of soft, dark hair.

# II.

**Port Angeles. — Indian "Hunter" and his Wife. — Sailor's Funeral. — Incantation. — Indian Graves. — Chief Yeomans. — Mill Settlements. — Port Gamble Trail. — Canoe Travel. — The *Memaloost*. — Tommy and his Mother. Olympic Range. — Ediz Hook. — Mrs. S. and her Children. — Grand Indian Wedding. — Crows and Indians.**

PORT ANGELES, WASHINGTON TERRITORY,
July 20, 1865.

WE reached here day before yesterday, very early in the morning. We were called to the forward deck; and before us was a dark sea-wall of mountains, with misty ravines and silver peaks, — the Olympic Range, a fit home for the gods.

A fine blue veil hung over the water, between us and the shore; and, the air being too heavy for the smoke of the Indian village to rise, it lay in great curved lines, like dim, rainbow-colored serpents, over sea and land.

I thought it was the loveliest place I had ever seen. The old Spanish explorers must have thought so too, as they named it "Port of the Angels."

We found that the path to our house was an Indian trail, winding about a mile up the bluff from the beach; the trees shutting overhead, and all about us a drooping white spirea, a most bridal-looking flower. Here and there, on some precipitous bank, was the red Indian-flame. Every once in a while, we came to a little opening looking down upon the sea; and the sound of it was always in our ears. At last we reached a partially cleared space, and there stood the house; behind it a mountain range, with snow filling all the ravines, and, below, the fulness and prime of summer. We are nearly at the foot of the hills, which send us down their snow-winds night and morning, and their ice-cold water. Between us and them are the fir-trees, two hundred and fifty and three hundred feet high; and all around, in the burnt land, a wilderness of bloom, — the purple fireweed, that grows taller than our heads, and in the richest luxuriance, of the same color as the Alpine rose, — a beautiful foreground for snowy hills.

The house is not ready for us. We are obliged at present, for want of a chimney, to stop with our nearest neighbor. But we pay it frequent visits. Yesterday, as we sat there, we received a call from two Indians, in extreme undress. They walked in with perfect freedom, and sat down on the floor. We shall endeavor to procure from Victoria a dictionary of the Haidah, Chinook, and other Indian languages, by the aid of which we shall be able to receive such visitors in a more satisfactory manner. At present, we can only smile very much at them. Fortunately, on this occasion, our carpenter was present, who told us that the man was called "Hunter," which served as an introduction. Hunter took from the woman a white bag, in which was a young wild bird, and put it into my hands. The carpenter said that this Indian had done some work for him, bringing up lumber from the beach, etc., and had come for his pay; that he would not take a white man's word for a moment, but if, in making an agreement with him, a white man gave him a little bit of paper with *any thing* written on it, he was perfectly satisfied, and said, "You my *tilikum* [relation] — I wait."

The neighbor with whom we are stopping says, that, the night before we came, a wildcat glared in at her as she sat at her window.

It looks very wild here, the fir-trees are so shaggy. I think the bears yet live under them. Many of the trees are dead. When the setting sun lights up the bare, pointed trunks, the great troops of firs look like an army with spears of gold, climbing the hills.

JULY 30, 1865.

To-day, as we were descending by the trail from the bluff to the beach, we saw a funeral procession slowly ascending the wagon-road. It came from the Sailors' Hospital. We waited until it passed. The cart containing the coffin was drawn by oxen, and followed by a little white dog and a few decrepit sailors. There was no sign of mourning, but a reverent look in their faces. The body had been wrapped in a flag by brotherly hands. The deep music of the surf followed them, and the dark fir-branches met overhead.

In California, the poorest of people, by the competition of undertakers, are furnished, at low rates, with the use of silver-mounted hearses and nodding plumes, a shrouding of crape, and a long line of carriages. Even those who have really loved the one who is gone seem, in some incomprehensible way, to find a solace in these manifestations, and would have considered this sailor's solitary funeral the extreme of desolation. But Nature took him gently to her bosom; the soft sky and the fragrant earth seemed to be calling him home.

We found by inquiry that it was the funeral of an entirely unknown sailor, who had not even any distant friends to whom he wished messages sent. His few possessions he left for the use of the children of the place, and quietly closed his eyes among strangers, returning peacefully to the unknown country whence he came.

AUG. 2, 1865.

We went this morning to an Indian *Tamáhnous* (incantation), to drive away the evil spirits from a sick man. He lay on a mat, surrounded by women, who beat on instruments made by stretching deer-skin over a frame, and accompanied the noise thus produced by a monotonous wail. Once in a while it became quite stirring, and the sick man seemed to be improved by it. Then an old man crept in stealthily, on all-fours, and, stealing up to him, put his mouth to the flesh, here and there, apparently sucking out the disease.

AUG. 17, 1865.

Hunter stopped to rest to-day on our doorsteps. He had a haunch of elk-meat on his back, one end resting on his head, with a cushion of green fern-leaves. He called me "*Closhe tum-tum*" (Good Heart), and gave me a great many beautiful smiles.

We find that there are a number of canoes suspended in the large fir-trees on some of our land, with the mummies of Indians in them. These are probably the bodies of chiefs, or persons of high rank. There is also a graveyard on the beach, which is gay with bright blankets, raised like flags, or spread out and nailed upon the roofs over the graves, and myriads of tin pans: we counted thirty on one grave. A looking-glass is one of the choicest of the decorations. On one we noticed an old trunk, and others were adorned with rusty guns.

Last night there came a prolonged, heavy, booming sound, different from any thing we had heard before. In the morning we saw that there had been a great landslide on the mountain back of us, bringing down rocks and trees.

AUG. 30, 1865.

Yeomans, an old Indian chief, the *Tyce* of the Flat-heads at Port Angeles, came to see us to-day. He pointed to himself, and said, "Me all the same white man;" explaining that he did not paint his face, nor drink whiskey. Mrs. S., at the light-house, said that she had frequently invited him to dinner, and that he handled his napkin with perfect propriety: although he is often to be seen sitting cross-legged on the sand, eating his meal of sea-urchins.

He is very dramatic, and described to us by sounds only, without our understanding any of the words, how wild the water was at Cape Flattery, and how the ships were rocked about there. It was thrilling to hear the sounds of the winds as he represented them: I felt as if I were in the midst of a great storm.

His little tribe appear to have great respect for his authority as a chief, and show a proper deference towards him. He is a mild and gentle ruler, and not overcome by the pride and dignity of his position. He is always ready to assist in dragging our boat on to the beach, and does not disdain the dime offered him in compensation for the service.

His son, a grown man, no longer young, who introduced himself to us as "Mr. Yeomans's son," and who appears to have no other designation, is much more of a wild Indian than the old man. Sometimes I see him at night, going out with his *klootchman* in their little canoe; she, crouched in her scarlet blanket at one end, holding the dark sail, and the great yellow moon shining on them.

I used to wonder, when we first came here, what their interests were, and what they were thinking about all the time. Little by little we find out. To-night he came in to tell us that there was going to be a great *potlach* at the coal-mines, where a large quantity of *iktas* would be given away, — tin pans, guns, blankets, canoes, and money. How his eyes glistened as he described it! It seems that any one who aspires to be a chief must first give a *potlach* to his tribe, at which he dispenses among them all his possessions.

This afternoon, as I sat at my window, my attention was attracted by a little noise. I looked up; and there was a beautiful young Indian girl, holding up a basket of fruit, of the same color as her lips and cheeks. It was a delicious wild berry that grows here, known as the red huckleberry. Mrs. S. knew her, and told me that she was the daughter of the old chief, lately betrothed to a Cape-Flattery Indian.

SEPT. 20, 1865.

Everywhere about Puget Sound and the adjoining waters are little arms of the sea running up into the land, like the fiords of Northern Europe. Many of them have large sawmills at the head. We have been travelling about, stopping here and there at the little settlements around the mills. We were everywhere most hospitably received. All strangers are welcomed as guests. Every thing seems so comfortable, and on such a liberal scale, that we never think of the people as poor, although the richest here have only bare wooden walls, and a few articles of furniture, often home-made. It seems, rather, as if we had moved two or three generations back, when no one had any thing better; or, as if we might perhaps be living in feudal times, these great mill-owners have such authority in the settlements. Some of them possess very large tracts of land, have hundreds of men in their employ, own steamboats and hotels, and have large stores of general merchandise, in connection with their mill-business. They sometimes provide amusements for the men, — little dramatic entertainments, etc., — to keep them from resorting to drink; and encourage them to send for their families, and to make gardens around their houses.

The house where we stopped at Port Madison was very attractive. The maple-trees had been cut down to build it; but life is so vigorous here, that they grew up under the porch, and then, as they became taller, came outside, and curved up around it, so that it was a perfect nest. The maple here is not just like the Eastern tree, but has a larger, darker leaf. Inside, the rooms were large and low, with great fireplaces filled with flaming logs, that illuminated them brilliantly.

We began our expedition round the Sound in a plunger, — the most atrocious little craft ever constructed. Its character is well expressed by its name. These boats are dangerous enough in steady hands; but, as they are exceedingly likely to be becalmed, the danger is very much increased from the temptation to drink that seems always to assail the captain and men in these wearisome delays.

To avoid waiting two or three days at Port Madison for the steamer, we determined to cross to the next port by an Indian trail through the woods; though we were told that it was very rough travelling, and that no white woman had ever crossed there, and, also, that we might have to take circuitous routes to avoid fires. We started early in the morning, allowing the whole day for the journey. We passed through one of the burnt regions, where the trees were still standing, so gray and spectral that it was like a strange dream. Farther along we heard a prolonged, mournful sound, that we could not account for; but, in a little while, we came to where the bright flames were darting from the trunks and branches, and curling around them. The poor old trees were creaking and groaning, preparatory to falling. We were obliged, occasionally, to abandon the trail; or, rather, it abandoned us, being burnt through. Off the path, the underbrush was almost impassable; the vine-maple, with crooked stems and tangled branches, with coarse briers and vines, knit every thing together. It seemed more like a tropical than a northern forest, there were so many glossy evergreen leaves. We recognized among them the holly-leaf barberry (known also as the Oregon grape), one of the most beautiful of shrubs. Its pretty clusters of yellow flowers were withered, and its fruit not yet ripe. We found also the sallal, — the Indian's berry, — the salmon-colored raspberry, and the coral-red huckleberry. Occasionally we heard the scream of a hawk, or the whirring of great wings above our heads; but, for the most part, we tramped on in perfect silence. The woods were too dark and dense for small birds.

It was curious to notice how much some of the little noises sounded like whispers, or like footsteps. There was hardly a chance that there could be any other human beings there besides ourselves. It recalled to me the Indian's dread of *skookums* (spirits) in the deep woods. To him, the mere flutter of a leaf had a meaning; the sighing of the wind was intelligible language. So many generations of Indians had crossed that trail, and so few white people, I felt as if some subtile aroma of Indian spirit must linger still about the place, and steal into our thoughts. Occasionally an owl stirred in the thicket beside us, or we caught a glimpse of the mottled beauty of a snake gliding across our path. The great boom and crash of the falling trees startled us, until we were used to it, and understood it.

Whenever we left the trail, we felt some doubt lest we might not find it again, or might happen upon an impassable stream that would cut us off from farther progress; not feeling quite equal to navigating with a pole on a snag, after the fashion of the Indians.

Near sunset, when the woods began to grow darker around us, we saw a bird, about as large as a robin, with a black crescent on his breast. His song was very different from that of the robin, and consisted of five or six notes, regularly descending in minor key. It thrilled me to hear it in the solitary woods: it was like the wail of an Indian spirit.

It began to be quite a serious question to us, what we were to do for the night; as how near or how far Port Gamble might be, we could not tell. There was no possibility of our climbing the straight fir-trees, with branches high overhead; and to stop on the ground was not to be thought of, for fear of wild beasts. We hastened on, but the trail became almost undistinguishable before the lights of Port Gamble appeared below us. As we descended to the settlement, we were met with almost as much excitement on the part of the mill people, who had never crossed the trail, as if we had risen from the water, or floated down from the sky, among them.

We take great satisfaction in the recollection of this one day of pure Indian life.

The next day we decided to try a canoe. We should not have ventured to go alone with the Indians, not understanding their talk; but another passenger was to go with us, who represented that he had learned the only word it would be necessary to use. He explained to us, after we started, that the word was "*hyac*," which meant "hurry up;" the only danger being that we should not reach Port Townsend before dark, as they were apt to proceed in so leisurely a way when left to themselves. After a while, the bronze paddlers — two *siwashes* (men) and two *klootchmen* (women) — began to show some abatement of zeal in their work, and our fellow-passenger pronounced the talismanic word, with some emphasis; whereat they laughed him to scorn, and made some sarcastic remarks, half

Chinook and half English, from which we gathered that they advised him, if he wanted to reach Port Townsend before dark, to tell the sun to stop, and not tell them to hurry up. We could only look on, and admire their magnificent indifference. They stopped whenever they liked, and laughed, and told stories. The sky darkened in a very threatening way, and a heavy shower came on; but it made not the slightest difference to them. After it was over, there was a splendid rainbow, like the great gate of heaven. This animated the Indians, and their spirits rose, so that they began to sing; and we drifted along with them, catching enough of their careless, joyous mood, not to worry about Port Townsend, although we did not reach the wharf till two or three hours after dark.

A day or two after, we found, rather to our regret, that we should be obliged to take a canoe again, from Port Discovery. The intoxicated "Duke of Wellington" — an Indian with a wide gold band round his hat, and a dilapidated naval uniform — came down, and invited us to go in his sloop. We politely declined the offer, and selected Tommy, the only Indian, we were told, who did not drink. With the aid of some of the bystanders, we asked his views of the weather. He said there would undoubtedly be plenty of wind, and plenty of rain, but it would not make any difference: he had mats enough, and we could stop in the woods. But, as we had other ideas of comfort, we waited two days; and, as the weather was still unsettled, we took the precaution, before starting, to give him his directions for the trip: "*Halo* wind, Port Angeles; *hyiu* wind, Dungeness," meaning that we were to have the privilege of stopping at Dungeness if it should prove too stormy to go on. So he and his little *klootchman*, about as big as a child of ten, took us off. When we reached the portage over which they had to carry the canoe, he pointed out the place of the *memaloost* (the dead). I see the Indians often bury them between two bodies of water, and have wondered if this had any significance to them. I have noticed, too, that their burial-places have always wild and beautiful surroundings. At this place, the blue blankets over the graves waved in the wind, like the wings of some great bird. A chief was buried here; and some enormous wooden figures, rudely carved, stood to guard him. They looked old and worn. They had long, narrow eyes, high cheek-bones, and long upper lips, like true Indians, with these features somewhat exaggerated.

We tried to talk with Tommy a little about the *memaloost.* He said it was all the same with an Indian, whether he was *memaloost*, or on the *illahie* (the earth); meaning that he was equally alive. We were told at the store, that Tommy still bought sugar and biscuits for his child who had died.

When we reached the other side of the portage, the surf roared so loud, it seemed frightful to launch the canoe in it; but Tommy praised R. as *skookum* (very strong) in helping to conduct it over. He seemed much more good-natured than the Indians we had travelled with before. He smiled at the loon floating past us, and spoke to it.

When we reached Dungeness, he represented that it would be very rough outside, in the straits. So he took us to a farmhouse. I began to suspect his motive, when I saw that there was a large Indian encampment there, and he pointed to some one he said was all the same as his mamma. It was the exact representation of a sphinx,—an old gray creature lying on the sand, with the upper part of her body raised, and her lower limbs concealed by her blanket. I expected to see Tommy run and embrace her: but he walked coolly by, without giving her any greeting whatever; and she remained perfectly imperturbable, never stirred, and her expression did not change in the least. I was horror-stricken, but afterwards altered my views of her, and came to the conclusion that she was a good, kind mother, only that it was their way to refrain from all appearance of emotion. When we started the next morning, she came down to the canoe with the little *klootchman*, loaded with presents, which she carried in a basket on her back, supported by a broad band round her head, — smoking-hot venison, and a looking-glass for the child's grave, among them. The old lady waded into the water, and pushed us off with great energy and strong ejaculations.

As we approached Port Angeles, we had a fine view of the Olympic Range of mountains, — shining peaks of silver in clear outline; later, only dark points emerging from seas of yellow light. Little clouds were drawn towards them, and seemed like birds hovering over them, sometimes lighting, or sailing slowly off.

EDIZ HOOK LIGHT, Sept. 23, 1865.

This light-house is at the end of a long, narrow sand-spit, known by the unpoetical name of Ediz Hook, which runs out for three miles into the Straits of Fuca, in a graceful curve, forming the bay of Port Angeles. Outside are the roaring surf and heavy swell of the sea; inside that slender arm, a safe shelter.

In a desolate little house near by, lives Mrs. S., whose husband was recently lost at sea. She is a woman who awakens my deepest wonder, from her being so able to dispense with all that most women depend on. She prefers still to live here (her husband's father keeps the light), and finds her company in her great organ. One of the last things her husband did was to order it for her, and it arrived after his death. I think the sailors must hear it as they pass the light, and wonder where the beautiful music comes from. There is something very soft and sweet in her voice and touch.

Sometimes I see the four children out in the boat. The little girls are only four and six years old, yet they handle the oars with ease. As I look at their bare bright heads in the sunshine, they seem as pretty as pond-lilies. I feel as if they were as safe, they are so used to the water.

**Port Angeles, Oct. 1, 1865.**

Port Angeles has been the scene of a grand ceremony, — the marriage of Yeomans's daughter to the son of a Makah chief. Many of the Makah tribe attended it. They came in a fleet of fifty canoes,—large, handsome boats, their high pointed beaks painted and carved, and decorated with gay colors. The chiefs had eagle-feathers on their heads, great feather-fans in their hands, and were dressed in black bear-skins. Our Flat-heads in their blankets looked quite tame in contrast with them. They approached the shore slowly, standing in the canoes. When they reached the landing in front of Yeomans's ranch, the congratulations began, with wild gesticulations, leapings, and contortions. They were tall, savage-looking men. Some of them had rings in their noses; and all had a much more primitive, uncivilized look, than our Indians on the Sound. I could hardly believe that the gentlemanly old Yeomans would deliver up his pretty daughter to the barbarians that came to claim her, and looked to see some one step forward and forbid the banns; but the ceremony proceeded as if every thing were satisfactory. There may be more of the true old Indian in him than I imagined; or perhaps this is a political movement to consolidate the friendship of the tribes. When they landed, they formed a procession, bearing a hundred new blankets, red and white, as a *potlach* to the tribe. They brought also some of the much-prized blue blankets, reserved for special ceremonies and the use of chiefs.

What occurred inside the lodge, we could not tell; but were quite touched at seeing Yeomans's son take the flag from his dead sister's grave, and plant it on the beach at high-water mark, as if it were a kind of participation, on the part of the dead girl, in the joy of the occasion.

OCT. 5, 1865.

Flocks of crows hover continually about the Indian villages. The most proverbially suspicious of all birds is here familiar and confiding. The Indian exercises superstitious care over them, but whether from love or fear we could never discover. It is very difficult to find out what an Indian believes. We have sometimes heard that they consider the crows their ances tors. It is a curious fact, that the Indians, in talking, make so much use of the palate, — *kl* and other guttural sounds occurring so often, — and that the crow, in his deep "caw, caw," uses the same organ. It may be significant of some psychological relationship between them.

# III.

**Indian Chief Seattle. — Frogs and Indians. — Spring Flowers and Birds. — The Red *Tamáhnous*. — The little Pend d'Oreille. — Indian Legend. — From Seattle to Fort Colville. — Crossing the Columbia River Bar. — The River and its Surroundings. — Its Former Magnitude. — The Grande Coulée. — Early Explorers, Heceta, Meares, Vancouver, Grey. — Curious Burial-place. — Chinese Miners. — Umatilla. — Walla Walla. — Sage-brush and Bunch-grass. — Flowers in the Desert. — "Stick" Indians. — Klickatats. — Spokane Indian. — Snakes. — Dead Chiefs. — A Kamas Field. — Basaltic Rocks.**

SEATTLE, WASHINGTON TERRITORY,
Nov. 5, 1865.

WE saw here a very dignified Indian, old and poor, but with something about him that led us to suspect that he was a chief. We found, upon inquiry, that it was Seattle, the old chief for whom the town was named, and the head of all the tribes on the Sound. He had with him a little brown sprite, that seemed an embodiment of the wind, — such a swift, elastic little creature, — his great-grandson, with no clothes about him, though it was a cold November day. To him, motion seemed as natural as rest.

Here we first saw Mount Rainier. It was called by the Indians *Tacoma* (The nourishing breast). It is also claimed that the true Indian name is *Tahoma* (Almost to heaven). It stands alone, nearly as high as Mont Blanc, triple-pointed, and covered with snow, most grand and inaccessible-looking.

We have a great laurel-tree beside our house. It looks so Southern, it is strange to see it among the firs. It has a dark outer bark, and a soft inner skin; both of which are stripped away by the tree in growing, and the trunk and branches are left bare and flesh-colored. It has glossy evergreen leaves, and bright red berries, that look very cheerful in contrast with the snow.

April 6, 1866.

The frogs have begun to sing in the marsh, and the Indians in their camps. How well their voices chime together! All the bright autumn days, we used to listen to the Indians at sunset; but after that, we heard no sound of them for several months. They sympathize too much with Nature to sing in the winter. Now the warm, soft air inspires them anew. All through the cold and rainy months, as I looked out from my window, there was always the little black figure in the canoe, as free and as unembarrassed by any superfluities as the birds that circled around it. It seemed a mistake, when the most severe weather came, for them to have made no preparation whatever to meet it. It drove the women into our houses, with their little bundles of "fire-sticks" (pitch-wood) to sell. I offered one of them a pair of shoes; but she pointed to the snow, and said it was "hot," and that it would make her feet too cold to wear shoes.

We were told, before we came here, that this climate was like that of Asia; and now an Asian flower has come to confirm it. The marshes are all gay with it: it is the golden club. The botany calls it the Orontium, because it grows on the banks of the Orontes; and it is very Asian-looking. It has a great wrapper, like the rich yellow silk in which the Japanese brought their presents to President Lincoln. It is a relation to the calla-lily, but is larger.

The very last day of winter, as if they could not possibly wait a day longer, great flocks of meadow-larks came, and settled down on the field next to us. They are about as large as robins, and have a braided work of black-and-gold to trim off their wings, and a broad black collar on their orange breasts. They appear to have a very agreeable consciousness of being in the finest possible condition. The dear old robins look rather faded beside them. With them came the crimson-headed linnets. In trying to identify these little birds from our books, I found that great confusion had prevailed in regard to them, because their nuptial plumage differs so much from their ordinary dress. These darlings blushed all over with life and joy, which told me their secret.

April 30, 1866.

In the winter we were told, that, when the spring came fully on, the Indians would have the "*Red Tamáhnous*," which means "love." A little, gray old woman appeared yesterday morning at our door, with her cheeks all aglow, as if her young blood had returned. Besides the vermilion lavishly displayed on her face, the crease at the parting of her hair was painted the same color. Every article of clothing she had on was bright and new. I looked out, and saw that no Indian had on any thing but red. Even old blind Charley, whom we had never seen in any thing but a black blanket, appeared in a new one of scarlet. But I was most touched by the change in this woman, because she is, I suppose, the oldest creature that I ever looked at. Nothing but a primeval rock ever seemed to me so old; and when we had seen her before, she was like a mummy generally in her clothing. These most ancient creatures have their little stiff legs covered with a kind of blue cloth, sewed close round them, just like the mummy-wrappings I have seen at Barnum's Museum. She has more vivacity and animation than any one else I ever saw. If anybody has a right to bright cheeks, she has. I like the Indians' painting themselves, for in them it is quite a different thing from what it is in fashionable ladies. They do it to show how they feel, not commonly expressing their emotions in words.

This woman, who is a Pend d'Oreille, has the most extraordinary power of modulation in her voice. The Indians, by prolonging the sound of words, add to their force, and vary their meaning; so that the same word signifies more or less, according as it is spoken quickly or slowly. She has such a searching voice, especially when she is attempting to convict me of any subterfuge or evasion, that I have to yield to her at once. The Indians have no word, as far as I can learn, for "busy." So, when I cannot entertain her, I have to make the nearest approach I can to the truth, and tell her I am sick, or something of that kind; but nothing avails, with her, short of the absolute truth.

She is so very fantastic and entertaining, that I should cultivate her acquaintance more, if it were not for this deficiency in the language, which makes it impossible to convey the idea to her when I want to get rid of her. As old as she is, she still carries home the great sacks of flour — a hundred pounds — on her back, superintends the salmon-fishery for the family, takes care of the *tenas men* (children), and looks after affairs in general.

MAY 10, 1866.

We walked out to Lake Union, and found an Indian and his wife living in a tree. The most primitive of the Indians, the old gray ones, who look the most interesting, do not commonly speak the Chinook at all, or have any intercourse with the whites. On the way there, we found the peculiar rose that grows only on the borders of the fir-forest, the wild white honeysuckle, and the glossy *kinni-kinnick* — the Indian tobacco.

We saw a nest built on the edge of the lake, rising and falling with the water, but kept in place by the stalks of shrubs about it. A great brown bird, with spotted breast, rose from it. I recognized it as the dabchick. The Indians say that this bird was once a human being, wife to an Indian with whom she quarrelled. He was transformed to the great blue heron, and stalks about the marshes. With the remnant of her woman's skill, she makes these curious nests, in sheltered nooks, on the edges of lakes. She dived below the water, and we peeped in at her babies. Their floating nest was overhung by white spirea. They had silver breasts, and pale blue bills. I wondered that their little bleating cry did not call her back; but, though below the water, she seemed to know that we were near, and as long as we lingered about she would not return.

We are going on a long journey to the north, part of it over a desert table-land, where for four days there will be no house,—a part of the country frequented by the Snake River Indians and the Nez Perces, who are inclined to be hostile. It is near the territory of the Pend d'Oreilles. I have seen one of them, with a pretty, graceful ornament in her ear.

FORT COLVILLE, WASHINGTON TERRITORY,
June 8, 1866.

We travelled by steamer from Seattle to Portland, thence by a succession of steamers as far as Wallulla. We then took the stage for Walla Walla, at which point public accommodation for travel ceases. We stopped there two or three days, seeking a conveyance across the country to this point; and finally secured a wagoner, who agreed to transport us and our luggage for a hundred dollars, the distance being two hundred miles.

The most interesting part of the journey was the passage of the Columbia. The bar at the mouth of the river is a great hinderance to its free navigation; and vessels are often detained for days, and even weeks, waiting for a favorable opportunity to cross. We waited five days outside in the fog, hearing all the time the deep, solemn warning of the breakers, to keep off. Our steadfast captain, as long as he could see nothing, refused to go on, knowing well the risk, though he sent the ship's boats out at times to try to get his bearings. In all that time, the fog never once lifted so that he could get the horizon-line. At the end of the fifth day, he entered in triumph, with a clear view of the river, the grandest sight I have ever seen. The passengers seemed hardly to dare to breathe till we were over the bar. Some of them had witnessed a frightful wreck there a few years before, when, after a similar waiting in the fog for nearly a week, a vessel attempted to enter the river, and struck on the bar. She was seen for two days from Astoria, but the water was so rough that no life-boat could reach her. The passengers embarked on rafts, but were swept off by the sea.

As we passed into the river, I sat on deck, looking about. All at once I felt a heavy thump on my back, and a wave broke over my head,—a pretty rough greeting from the sea. It seems that we slightly grounded, but were off in an instant.

I had long looked forward to the wonderful experience of seeing this immense river, seven miles broad, rolling seaward, and the great line of breakers at the bar; but no one can realize, without actually seeing it, how much its grandeur is enhanced by the surroundings of interminable forest, and the magnificence of its snow-mountains. The character of the river itself is in accordance with every thing about it, especially where it breaks through the Cascade Mountains in four miles of rapids; and still higher up, shut between basaltic walls, rushes with deafening roar through the narrow passage of the Dalles, where it is compressed into one-eighth of its width. For a long time I could not receive any other sensation, nor admit any other thought, but of its terrific strength. The Indians say that in former times the river flowed smoothly where are now the whirling rapids of the Cascades, but that a land-slide from the banks dammed up the stream, and produced this great change. How many generations have repeated the account of this wonderful occurrence, from one to another, to bring it down to our times! This is now accepted by scientific men as undoubtedly the fact.

It is hard to conceive the idea of the geologists, that this is only the remnant of a vastly greater Columbia, that formerly occupied not only its present bed, but other channels, now abandoned, including the Grande Coulée, between whose immense walls it poured a current ten miles broad at the mouth; and that the water was at some time one or two thousand feet above the present level of the river, as shown by the terraces along its banks, and fragments of drift caught in fissures of the rock. The Grande Coulée is like an immense roofless ruin, extending north and south for fifty miles. Strange forms of rock are scattered over the great bare plain. To the Indians, it is the home of evil spirits. They say there are rumblings in the earth, and that the rocks are hot, and smoke. Thunder and lightning, so rare elsewhere on the western coast, are here more common. The evidences of volcanic action are everywhere apparent, — in the huge masses and curious columns of basaltic and trap-rock, the lava-beds through which the rivers have found their way, and the powdery alkaline soil. The marks of glaciers are also as distinct in the bowlders, and the scooping-out of the beds of lakes. The gravelly prairies between the Columbia and Puget Sound, and the Snoqualmie, Steilaguamish, and other flats, show that the Sound was formerly of much more extensive proportions than at present.

The Columbia was first discovered on the 15th of August, 1775, by Bruno Heceta, a Spanish explorer, who found an opening in the coast. from which rushed so strong a current as to prevent his entering. He concluded that it was the mouth of some great river, or possibly the Straits of Fuca, which might have been erroneously marked on his chart. As this was the anniversary of the Assumption of the Virgin Mary, he named the opening *Enseñada de Asuncion* (Assumption Inlet); and it was afterwards called, in the charts published in Mexico, *Enseñada de Heceta*, and *Rio de San Roque*. He gave to the point on the north side the name of Cape *San Roque;* and, to that on the south, Cape *Frondoso* (Leafy Cape).

Meares, in 1788, gave the name of Cape Disappointment to the northern point, owing to his not being able to make the entrance of the river, and the mouth he called Deception Bay, and asserted that there was no such river as the St. Roc, as laid down in the Spanish charts.

Vancouver also, when exploring the Pacific coast in 1792, passed by this great stream, without suspecting that there was a river of any importance there. He noticed the line of breakers, and concluded, that, if there was any river, it must be unnavigable, from shoals and reefs. He had made up his mind, that all the streams flowing into the Pacific between the fortieth and forty-eighth parallels of latitude were mere brooks, insufficient for vessels to navigate, and not worthy his attention.

Capt. Grey, who reached the place shortly after, with keener observation and deeper insight, saw the indications of a great river there, and after lying outside for nine days, waiting a favorable opportunity to enter, succeeded in doing so on the 11th of May, 1792, being the first to accomplish that feat, and explored the lower portion of it. He gave to the river and to the southern point the names they now bear.

Vancouver failed in the same way to discover the Fraser, the great river of British Columbia, although he actually entered the delta of the river, and sailed about among the sand-banks, naming one of them Sturgeon Bank; while the Spanish explorers, who were there about the same time, recognized the fact of its existence far out at sea, in the irregular currents, the sand-banks, the drift of trees and logs, and also in the depression in the Cascade Mountains, which marks its channel.

In 1805 Lewis and Clarke, who reached the mouth of the Columbia that year, found that the Indians called the river "*Shocatilcum*" (friendly water).

Tourists have not yet discovered what a wonderful country this is for sight-seeing, fortunately for us. On our passage up the Columbia, after leaving Portland, we sat for two or three days, almost alone, on the deck of the steamer, with nothing to break the silence but the deep breathing of the boat, which seemed like its own appreciation of it; and sailed past the great promontories, some of them a thousand feet high, and watched the slender silver streams that fall from the rocks, and felt that we were in a new world, — new to us, but older and grander than any thing we had ever seen.

We were shown a high, isolated rock, rising far above the water, on which was a scaffolding, where, for many generations, the Indians had deposited their dead. They were wrapped in skins, tied with cords of grass and bark, and laid on mats. Their most precious possessions were placed beside them, first made unserviceable for the living, to secure their remaining undisturbed. The bodies were always laid with the head toward the west, because the *memaloose illahie* (land of the dead) lay that way.

In the instincts of children and of uncivilized people, there seems something to trust. This idea of Heaven's lying toward the west appears to have been held by the New-England Indians also, and is expressed in Whittier's lines, —

"O mighty Sowanna!
Thy gateways unfold,
From thy wigwam of sunset
Lift curtains of gold!
Take home the poor spirit whose journey is o'er —
*Mat wonck kunna-monce!* We see thee no more!"

The Chinese have also the "peaceful land in the west," lying far beyond the visible universe.

Farther up the river, we passed some abandoned diggings, where little colonies of patient, toilsome Chinamen had established themselves, and were washing and sifting the earth discarded by previous miners; making, we were told, on the average, two or three cents to the pan. The

Chinaman regularly pays, as a foreigner (and is almost the only foreigner who does so), his mining-license tax to the State. He never seeks to interfere with rich claims, and patiently submits to being driven away from any neglected spot he may have chosen if a white man takes a fancy to it.

We stopped one night at Umatilla City, a cheerless little settlement at the junction of the Umatilla River with the Columbia, in the midst of a bleak, dreary waste of sand and sage-brush, without a sign of a tree in any direction, a perfect whirlwind blowing all the time. What could induce people to live there, I could not imagine.

We stopped a day or two at Walla Walla, where one of the early forts was established; the post having been transferred from Wallula, where it was called Fort "Nez Perces," from the Indians in that vicinity, who wore in their noses a small white shell, like the fluke of an anchor.

The journey from Walla Walla to Fort Colville occupied eleven days and nights, during which time we did not take a meal in a house, nor sleep in a bed. It was cold, rainy, and windy, a good deal of the time, but we enjoyed it notwithstanding. To wake up in the clear air, with the bright sky above us, when it was pleasant; and to reach at night the little oases of willows and birches and running streams where we camped, — was enough to repay us for a good deal of discomfort. At one of the camping-grounds, — Cow Creek, — a beautiful bird sang all night; it sounded like bubbling water.

For several days we saw only great sleepy-looking hills, stretching in endless succession, as far as the horizon extended, from morning till night, as if a billowy ocean had been suddenly transfixed in the midst of its motion. They have only thin vegetation on them, — not enough to disturb or conceal the beautiful forms, the curves which the waves leave on the hills they deposit. Their colors are very subdued, — pale salmon from the dead grass, or light green like a thin veil, with the red earth showing dimly through. There is no change in looking at them, but from light to shadow, as the clouds move over them.

We travelled, for a long distance, over sage-brush and alkali plains. In this part of the country, sage-brush is a synonym for any thing that is worthless. We found the little woody twigs of it available for our camping-fires; but its amazing toughness reminded me of a story told by Mr. Boller, in his book "Among the Indians." He was taking a band of mustang half-breeds from California to Montana, when, to his surprise, one of the mares presented him with a foal. Supposing it would be impossible for it to keep up with the party, he took out his revolver to shoot it. Twice he raised it, but the little fellow trotted along so cheerily that his heart failed him, and he returned it to the holster. The colt swam creeks breast-high for the horses, and travelled on with sublime indifference to every thing but the gratification of its keen little appetite. He resolved to take it through, thinking it would never do to destroy an animal of so much pluck, and named it "Sage-brush." It swam every stream, flinched from nothing, and arrived in good order in Montana, a distance of three hundred miles, having travelled every day from the time it was half an hour old. Its name was most appropriate, as an illustration of the character of the plant.

Intermixed with the wastes of sage-brush were patches of bunch-grass. The horses sniffed it with delight as luxuriant pasturage. It is curious to see how nature here acts in the interest of civilization. The old settlers told us that many acres formerly covered with sage-brush were now all bunch-grass. It is a peculiarity of the sage-brush, that fire will not spread in it. The bush which is fired will burn to the ground, but the next will not catch from it. The grass steals in among the sage-brush; and, when that is burned, it carries the fire from one bush to another. Although the grass itself is consumed, the roots strike deep; and it springs up anew, overrunning the dead sage-brush.

Then we came to the most barren country I ever saw, — nothing but broken, rusty, worm-eaten looking rocks, where the rattlesnakes live. But here grew the most beautiful flower, peach-blossom color. It just thrust its head out of the earth, and the long pink buds stretched themselves out over the dingy bits of rock; and that was all there was of it. We took some of the roots, which are bulbous, and shall try to furnish them with sufficient hardships to make them grow.

One night, while in this region, we camped on a hill where the cayotes came up and cried round us, which made it seem quite wild.

Wherever there was any soil, there was another little plant that was very pretty to notice, both for itself, and because of its adaptation to the climate in the dry season. It was coated with a delicate fur; and long after the hot sun was up, and when every thing else was dry, great diamonds of dew glistened in its soft hair. We saw a great many plants of the lupine family, in every variety of shade, from crimson, blue, and purple, to white.

On the last days we had all the time before us dark mountains, with snow on their summits, and troops of trees on their sides, and ravines with sun-lighted mists travelling through them. It was like getting into an inhabited country, to reach the trees again: they were almost like human beings, after what we had seen. The Spokane River divides the great treeless plain on the south from the timbered mountainous country to the north.

During this journey, we came upon various little bands of Indians, of different tribes. We noticed the superiority of the "stick" Indians (those who live in the woods) over those who live by the sea. The former have herds of horses, and hunt for their living. The Indians who live by fishing are of tamer natures, poor and degraded, compared to those of the interior.

We saw at Walla Walla some of the Klickatats, from the mountains. They were very bright and animated in their appearance, and wore fringed dresses and ornamented leggings, and moccasins of buffalo-skin. They were mounted upon fancy-colored and spotted horses, which they prize above all others. They presented such a striking contrast to the lazy Clalams on the Sound,—who used to say to us in reply to our inquiries as to their occupations and designs, "*Cultus nannitsh, cultus mitlight*" (look about and do nothing), as if that were their whole business all day long,—that I was reminded of what some of the early explorers said, that no two nations of Europe differed more widely from each other than the different tribes of Indians.

One day we met an Spokane Indian, of very striking appearance, with a face like Dante's, but with a happier expression. He was most becomingly clothed in white blankets, compactly folded about him, with two or three narrow red stripes across his bonnet of the same material, which had a red peaked border, completely encircling the face, like an Irishwoman's night-cap, or rather day-cap, but much more picturesque. He was scouring the hills and plains between the Snake and Spokane Rivers, mounted on a gay little pony, in search of stolen horses. Upon being questioned as to his abiding-place, he informed us that he did not live anywhere.

We saw some representatives of another tribe

of Indians, the Snakes. They call themselves Shoshones, which means only "inland Indians." The white people called them Snakes, probably because of their marvellous power of eluding pursuit, by crawling off in the long grass, or diving in the water. They seemed more wild and agile than any we had seen. The Snakes were a very numerous tribe when the traders first came among them. When questioned as to their number, by the agents of "The Great White Chief," they said, "It is the same as the stars in the sky." They were a proud, independent people, living mostly on the plains, hunting the buffalo. They kept no canoes; depending only on temporary rafts of bulrushes or willows, if not convenient to ford or swim across the streams. They were the only Indians of this part of the country who had any knowledge of working in clay, — their necessities obliging them to make rude jugs in which to carry water across the bare plains. The mountain Snakes were outlaws, enemies to all other tribes. They lived in bands, in rocky caverns; and were said to have a wonderful power of imitating all sounds of nature, from the singing of birds to the howling of wolves, — by this means diverting attention from themselves, and escaping detection in their roving, predatory expeditions.

When we reached the ferry on the Snake River, we saw some Indians swimming their horses across. They were a hunting-party of Spokanes and Nez Perces. Strapped on to one of the horses, with a roll of blankets, was a Nez Perces baby. This infant, though apparently not over a year and a half old, sat erect, grasping the reins, with as spirited and fearless a look as an old warrior's.

At one of the portages, we saw some graves of chiefs; the bodies carefully laid in east-and-west lines, and the opening of the lodge built over them was toward the sunrise. On a frame near the lodge were stretched the hides of their horses, sacrificed to accompany them to another world. The missionaries congratulate themselves that these barbarous ceremonies are no longer observed, that the Indian is weaned from his idea of the happy hunting-ground, and the sacrilegious thought of ever meeting his horse again is eradicated from his mind. I thought with satisfaction that the missionary really knows no more about the future than the Indian, who seems ill adapted to the conventional idea of heaven. For my part, I prefer to think of him, in the unknown future, as retaining something of his earthly wildness and freedom, rather than as a white-robed saint, singing psalms, and playing on a harp.

Between the Snake and the Spokane are several beautiful lakes. We met a hunter coming from one of them, who had shot a white swan. He said he found it circling round and round its dead mate, in so much distress that he thought it was a kindness to kill it.

We passed two great smoking mounds, and, on alighting to investigate, found that we were in the midst of a kamas-field, where a great many Indian women and children were busy digging the root, and roasting it in the earth.

Some of the old women wore the fringed skirt, made of cloth spun and woven from the soft inner bark of the young cedar, which they used to wear before blankets were introduced.

The Indians eat other roots beside the kamas, but that is the one on which they chiefly depend.. As soon as the snow is off the ground, they begin to search for a little bulbous root they call the *pohpoh.* It looks like a small onion, and has a dry, spicy taste. In May they get the *spatlam*, or bitter-root. This is a delicate white root, that dissolves in boiling, and forms a bitter jelly. The Bitter Root River and Mountains get their name from this plant. In June comes the kamas. It looks like a little hyacinth-bulb, and when roasted is as nice as a chestnut. We have seen it in blossom, when its pale-blue flowers covered the fields so closely that, at a little distance, we took it for a lake. One of the women, seeing our curiosity as we watched them, drew some of the bulbs out of the earth ovens, and handed them to us. As we tasted them, they explained that they were not ready to eat; that it would take two or three days to roast them sufficiently. This they live upon for two or three months; with the salmon, it is their chief article of food. The women stop at the kamas-grounds, while the men go to the fishing-stations.

In August they gather the choke-berry and service-berry, to dry for the winter. When they are reduced to great extremity for food, they sometimes boil and eat the moss and lichens on the trees, which the deer eats. Most of the work of digging the roots, and picking the berries, falls upon the women. On this account, a Spokane man in marrying joins the tribe of his wife, instead of her joining his tribe; thinking, if he takes her away from the places where she has been accustomed to find her roots and berries, she may not succeed, in a new place, in discovering them.

We saw, in the vicinity of the Pelouse River, some remarkable basaltic rocks, that looked like buildings with columns and turrets and bastions. Some of them were like my idea of the great kings' tombs of the Egyptians. The colors on them were often very Egyptian-like, — bright sulphur-yellow, and brown, and sometimes orange and dark red, — incrustations of lichen and weather-staining. We saw, also, walls of pentagonal columns of rock, packed closely together. Where the Pelouse enters the Snake River, are immense ledges of square blocks. When we camped there, and I lay down beneath them at night, "Swedish *trappa*, a stair," from the geological text-book, was always running in my mind, — this black trap-rock made such great steps that led up towards the sky.

We have seen here a splendid specimen of gold, which is to be sent to the Exposition at Paris. It is granulated, and sparkles as I never saw gold before. Some one suggests that a thin film of quartz may be crystallized over it.

Next week we hope to go up within sight of the whirlpools of Death's Rapids, a long distance above here, on the Columbia River. These rapids are so named on account of the number of persons who have been lost in attempting to navigate them. Their names are cut into the rocks at the side of the passage; their bodies have never been found.

## IV.

**Two Hundred Miles on the Upper Columbia. — Steamer "Forty-nine." — Navigation in a Cañon. — Pend d'Oreille River and Lake. — Rock Paintings. — Tributaries of the Upper Columbia. — Arrow Lakes. — Kettle Falls. — Salmon-catching. — Salmon-dance. — Goose-dance.**

FORT COLVILLE, July 20, 1866.

WE have just returned from a trip on the Columbia River, extending two hundred miles north into British Columbia, on the little steamer built in this vicinity for the purpose of carrying passengers and supplies to the Big Bend and other mines in the upper country. We did not get to the "Rapids of the Dead." The boat, this time, did not complete her ordinary trip. Some of the passengers came to the conclusion that the river was never intended to be navigated in places she attempted to run through. It is a very adventurous boat, called the "Forty-nine," being the first to cross that parallel, — the line separating Washington Territory from British Columbia. The more opposition she meets with, and the more predictions there are against her success, the more resolute she is to go through; on which account, we were kept three weeks on the way, the ordinary length of the passage being four days. I was surprised, when we came to the first of what was called the "bad water," to see the boat aim directly for it. It was much better, the captain said, to go "head on," than to run the risk of being carried in by an eddy. I never saw any river with such a tendency to whirl and fling itself about as the Upper Columbia has. It is all eddies, in places where there is the least shadow of a reason for it, and even where there is not; influenced, I suppose, by the adjoining waters. Some of these whirl-pits are ten or fifteen feet deep, measured by the trees that are sucked down into them.

The most remarkable part of the river is where it is compressed to one-sixth of its width, in passing through a mountain gorge three-quarters of a mile long. The current is so strong there, that it takes from four to six hours for the steamer to struggle up against it, and only one minute to come down. The men who have passed down through it, in small boats, say that it is as if they were shot from the mouth of a cannon.

When we reached this cañon, our real difficulties began. We attempted to enter it in the afternoon, but met with an accident which delayed us until the next morning. Meanwhile the river began to rise. It goes up very rapidly, fifty, sixty, I believe even seventy, feet, sometimes. We waited twelve days in the woods for it to subside. The captain cut us a trail with his axe; and we sat and looked at the great snow-fields up on the mountains, so brilliant that the whitest clouds looked dark beside them. The magnificence of the scenery made every one an artist, from the captain to the cook, who produced a very beautiful drawing of three snow-covered peaks, which he called "The Three Sisters."

Everybody grew very impatient; and at length, one night, the captain said he would try it the next morning, although he had never before been up when the water was so high. A heavy rain came on, lasting all night, so that it seemed rather desperate to attempt going through, if the river was too high the night before; and I could hardly believe it, when I heard the engineer getting up the steam to start. The wildest weather prevailed at this time, and on all important occasions. As soon as we went on board the boat, in first starting, a violent thunder-storm came on, lightning, hail, and rain; and a great pine-tree came crashing down, and fell across the bow of the boat. A similar storm came again the first time we tried to enter the cañon; and the drift it brought down so interfered with the steering, that it led to the accident before mentioned. On this last morning, there were most evident signs of disapproval all about us,—the sky perfect gloom, and the river continually replenishing its resources from the pouring rain, and strengthening itself against us. But we steamed up to the entrance of the cañon. Then the boat was fastened by three lines to the shore, and the men took out a cable six hundred feet in length, which they carried along the steep, slippery rocks, and fastened to a great tree. One of them rolled down fifty feet into the water, but was caught by his companions before he was whirled away. They then returned to the boat, let on all the steam, and began to wind up the cable on the capstan. With the utmost power of the men and steam, it was sometimes impossible to see any progress. Finally, however, that line was wound up; and the boat was again secured to the bank, and the cable put out the second time. This part of the passage was still more difficult; and, after the line was arranged, two men were left on shore with grappling-irons to keep it off the rocks, — a great, fine-looking one, who appeared equal to any emergency, and a little, common one, with sandy hair and a lobster-colored face and neck. We watched them intently; and, as we drew near, we saw that the line had caught on something beneath the surface of the water, so that they could not extricate it. The little man toiled vigorously at it, standing in the water nearly up to his head; but appeared to be feebly seconded by the big one, who remained on the rocks. It seemed as if the line would part from the strain, or the boat strike the next moment. The mate shouted and gesticulated to them; but no voice could be heard above the raging water, and they either could not understand his motions, or could not do as they were directed. The boat bore directly down upon them. Presently it seemed evident to us that the little man must sacrifice himself for the steamer; but I did not know how it looked to him, — people are all so precious to themselves. He stopped a second, then flung back his cap and pole, and threw himself under the boiling water. Up came the rope to the surface, but the man was gone. Instantly after, he scrambled up the bank; and the great magnificent man did nothing but clutch him on the back when he was safely out.

We had then wound up about two-thirds of the cable. Immediately after, this remarkable occurrence took place: The great heavy line came wholly up out of the water. A bolt flew out of the capstan, which was a signal for the men who were at work on it to spring out of the way. The captain shouted, "Cut the rope!" but that instant the iron capstan was torn out of the deck, and jumped overboard, with the cable attached to it. I felt thankful for it, for I knew it was the only thing that could put an end to our presumptuous attempt. I had felt that this rope would be a great snare to us in case of accident. Three of our four rudders were broken; but the remaining one enabled us to get into an eddy that carried us to a little cove, where we stopped to repair damages sufficiently to come down the river.

All day, the rain had never ceased; and the river had seemed to me like some of those Greek streams that Homer tells of, which had so much personal feeling against individuals. I felt as if we were going to be punished for an audacious attempt, instead of rewarded for what might otherwise have been considered a brave one. When the capstan disappeared, it was just as if some great river-god, with a whiff of his breath, or a snap of his fingers, had tossed it contemptuously aside. So we turned back defeated. But there was a great deal to enjoy, when we came to think of it afterwards, and were safely out of it. We had seen nothing so bold and rugged before. An old Scotchman, who knows more about it than any one else here, had said to us before we started, "That British Columbia is such a terrible country, very little can ever be known of it." But there was a great deal that was beautiful too. I was particularly struck with the manner in which the Pend d'Oreille springs into the Columbia. Glen Ellis Fall, gliding down in its swiftness, always seemed to me more beautiful than almost any thing else I ever saw. But this river is more demonstrative. It springs up, and falls again in showers of spray, and comes with great leaps out of the cañon, in a way that I cannot describe. There is in it more freedom and strength and delight than in any thing else I ever saw. Far to the south-east, this stream widens into Lake Pend d'Oreille. On this lake are the wonderful painted rocks, rising far above the water, upon which, at the height of several hundred feet, are the figures of men and animals, which the Indians say are the work of a race that preceded them. They are afraid to approach the rocks, lest the waters should rise in anger, and ingulf them. There are also hieroglyphic figures far up on the rocks of Lake Chelan, which is supposed to have once been an arm of the Columbia. These paintings or picture-writings must have been made when the water was so high in the lakes that they could be done by men in boats.

Most of the tributaries of the Upper Columbia are similar in character to the main stream, — wild, unnavigable rivers, flowing through deep cañons, and full of torrents and rapids. With Nature so vigorous and unsubdued about us, all conventionalities seemed swept away; and something fresh and strong awoke in us, as if it had long slumbered until the presence of its kindred in these mountain streams called it to consciousness, — something of the force and freedom of these wild, tireless Titans, that poured down their white floods to the sea.

Most of these streams rise in lakes, and in some part of their course spread again into one or more lakes; as, the Arrow Lakes of the Columbia, the Flat-head, Kootenay, Pend d'Oreille, and Cœur d'Alêne, and the beautiful string of lakes of the Okinakane, and many others.

As we passed through the Upper Arrow

Lake and Lower Arrow Lake, which lie in British Columbia, we had some splendid views of mountain scenery. The Upper Lake is thirty-three miles long, and three in width, crystalline water, surrounded by snow-covered peaks and precipices, and forests of pine and cedar. The second is sixteen miles below the first, forty-two miles in length, and two and a half wide. Innumerable arrows were sticking in the crevices of the rocks. Formerly every Indian who passed deposited an arrow, — intended probably as an offering to the spirit that rules over the chase, just as the Indian medicine-man, when he gathers his roots, makes an offering to the earth.

The Catholic missionaries were much surprised to find crosses erected sometimes in lonely places, and at first supposed some other priests must have preceded them; but learned that they were set up by the Indians, in honor of the moon, to induce her to favor their nightly expeditions for robbery or the chase.

JULY 22, 1866.

We have been on an excursion to Kettle Falls on the Columbia, where the river dashes over the huge rocks in a most picturesque way. These falls were called *La Chaudière* by the

Canadian *voyageurs*, because the pool below looks like a great boiling caldron. We noticed that limestone there replaced the black basalt, of which we had seen so much, the water falling over a tabular bed of white marble.

There we saw some Indians engaged in spearing salmon, as the fish were attempting to leap the falls, in their passage up the stream to their breeding-places. They do not always succeed in passing the falls at their first leap, sometimes falling back two or three times. Many of them are dashed on the rocks at the Cascades, and at other points where the river presents obstacles to their progress. An immense number become victims to the nets of the fishermen, and the traps and spears of the Indians; and those that escape these dangers, and reach the upper waters, are very much bruised and battered,—"spent salmon" they are called. After their long journey of six or seven hundred miles from the sea, it seems as if they would be filled with despair at the sight of these boiling cataracts. They refuse bait on the way, apparently never stopping for food, from the time they leave the salt water. Often with fins and tails so worn down as to be almost useless, their noses worn to the bone, their eyes sunken, sometimes wholly extinguished, they struggle on to the last gasp, to ascend the streams to their sources. In calm weather they swim near the surface, and close to the shore, to avoid the strong current; and they are so possessed with this one purpose, and so regardless of every thing about them, that the Indians catch hundreds of them by merely slipping the gaff-hook under their bodies, and lifting them out of the water, — selecting the best to preserve for food, and throwing aside those that they consider as worthless. These pale, emaciated creatures, I looked at with the greatest interest. How strong is the impulse that carries them through, in spite of these almost insurmountable obstacles! It is beyond our knowledge, why, in coming in from the sea, they pass certain streams to enter others; but this they are known to do, so perfectly do they understand the mysterious direction given them.

The early explorers witnessed many ceremonies among the Indians not now observed by them; as, the salmon-dance, to celebrate the taking of the first salmon in the river. When the earliest spring salmon was caught in the Columbia, the Indians were extremely particular in their dealings with it. No white man could obtain it at any price, lest, by opening it with a knife instead of a stone, he should drive all following salmon from the river. Certain parts must be eaten with the rising, and others with the falling, tide; and many other minute regulations carefully observed. After the salmon-berry ripened, they relaxed their vigilance, feeling that by that time the influx was secure.

The Gros Ventres celebrated the goose-dance, to remind the wild geese, as they left in the autumn, that they had had good food all summer, and must come back in the spring. This dance was performed by women, each one carrying a bunch of long seed-grass, the favorite food of the wild goose. They danced to the sound of the drum, circling about with shuffling steps.

# V.

**Old Fort Colville. — Angus McDonald and his Indian Family. — Canadian *Voyageurs*. — Father Joseph. — Hardships of the Early Missionaries. — The Cœurs d'Alêne and their Superstitions. — The Catholic Ladder. — Sisters of Notre Dame. — Skill of the Missionaries in instructing the Indians. — Father de Smet and the Blackfeet. — A Native Dance. — Spokanes. — Exclusiveness of the Cœurs d'Alêne. — Battle of Four Lakes. — The Yakima Chief and the Road-makers.**

FORT COLVILLE, July 25, 1866.

WE have been making a little visit to Old Fort Colville, one of the Hudson Bay stations, kept by Angus McDonald, an old Scotchman, who has been there for a great many years. He is an educated gentleman, of a great deal of character and intelligence; and his wife is an Indian woman, who cannot live more than half the year in the house, and has to wander about, the rest of it, with her *tilicums* (relations and friends).

It was interesting to see how this cultivated man, accustomed to the world as he had been, had adapted himself to life in this solitary spot on the frontier, with his Indian children for his only companions. He has about ten. In some of them the Scotch blood predominated, but in most the Indian blood was more apparent. The oldest son, a grown man, was a very dark Indian, decorated with wampum. Christine, the oldest daughter, resembled her father most. She kept house for him, because, as she explained to us, her mother could not be much in-doors. She spoke, too, of disliking to be confined. I asked her where she liked best to be; and she said, with the Blackfeet Indians, because they had the prettiest dances, and could do such beautiful bead-work; and described their working on the softened skins of elk, deer, and antelope, making dresses for chiefs and warriors. We had a sumptuous meal of Rocky-Mountain trout, buffalo-tongues, and pemmican. Although Christine was, in some respects, quite a civilized young lady, she occasionally betrayed her innocence of conventionalities, as when she came and whispered to me, before the meal was announced, what the chief dishes were to be. She mentioned, as one of the delicacies of the Blackfeet, berries boiled in buffalo-blood.

Mr. McDonald told us many stories about the Canadian *voyageurs* employed by the Hudson Bay Company, illustrating their power of endurance and their elastic temperament. One of their men, he said, was lost for thirty-five days in the woods, and finally discovered by the Indians, crawling on his hands and feet towards a brook, nearly exhausted, but still keeping up his courage. He asked us if we could conjecture how he had kept alive all that time, with no means whatever, outside of himself, to procure food. He had actually succeeded in making a fine net from his own hair, with which he caught small fishes, devouring them raw, accompanied by a little grass or moss; not daring to eat any roots or berries, lest they might be poisonous, as the country was new to him. These Canadians are as brown as Indians, from their constant exposure to the sun and wind, and have adapted themselves completely to Indian ways, wearing a blanket *capote*, leather trousers, moccasins, and a fur cap, with a bright sash or girdle to hold a knife and a tobacco-pouch. Their half-breed children are generally excellent canoe-men and hunters, with the vivacity of the father, and the endurance of the mother's race. Marcel Bernier, one of these French Canadians, was one of the early settlers in the Cowlitz Valley; and we have travelled with him between the Columbia River and Puget Sound, and once stopped at his house over night. . It was quite different from the common Indian houses; having pillow-cases trimmed with ruffles and lace, and great bear-skin mats on the floor. The baby slept in a little hammock swung from the ceiling. The family were devoted Catholics, and sung matins and vespers, and had pictures and images of saints about the room. We were quite impressed by the advance in civilization which the little admixture of French blood had brought.

Christine took us to see an ancient Indian woman, who remembers the country when there were no white people in it. She has the fifth generation of her children about her. She is wholly blind, her eyes mostly closed, only little bloodshot traces of them left. She sat serenely in the sunshine, hollowing out a little canoe of pine-bark for the youngest, two little girls who swam in the arm of the river before the tent-door.

We went with Christine also up on the bluff to see Father Joseph, a Catholic priest, who represented to me a new class of men, whom I had known before only in books. His eyes were as clear blue as Emerson's ideal ones, that tell the truth; and I knew he meant it, when he answered a question I asked him, in a way that surprised me, and which I should have taken, in some men, for cant. I asked him if it was not ever solitary there; and he said, "It is enough like my own home [Switzerland] for that, but all countries are alike to me. We have no home here below." For twenty-five years he has lived on the top of that hill, with only miserable Indians around him, who could repay him very little for all his efforts. In the Indian war, he was supposed to be so strongly on the side of the Indians, that the government agent, as I find by the printed report, recommended his removal; although he admitted that it was hard to say any thing against a man who had made such unbounded sacrifices for what he considered the good of the Indians. He had books in all languages on his shelves, and was very intelligent and courteous.

He described the condition of the country when the first little band of Jesuits, of whom he was one, entered upon the Oregon mission, — Oregon then extending east as far as the Rocky Mountains. They had often to travel through dark forests, into which the daylight never entered, and, axe in hand, make their own paths through the wilderness, sometimes crawling on all-fours through labyrinths of fallen trees, fording rivers where the water reached to their shoulders, travelling afterwards in their wet clothes, with swollen limbs, and moccasins soaked in blood from laceration of their feet by the thorns of the prickly pear, and lying down at night on their beds of brushwood, wrapped in their buffalo-robes. The Indians were full of curiosity to know what they were in search of, and listened with great interest when they attempted to talk with them. The first group that Father Joseph gathered about him sat all night to hear him, although they had come from hard labor of hunting and fishing, and digging roots. He said, that, however degraded they were, they were all eager to find some power superior to man.

The tribe among whom he first established himself — the Cœurs d'Alêne — were renowned among all the tribes for their belief in sorcery; and he experienced great difficulty in making an impression upon them, from the opposition of the medicine-men (jugglers). Among this tribe he found two relics held in great esteem, of which the Indians gave him this account: —

They said that the first white man they ever saw wore a spotted-calico shirt — which to them appeared like the small-pox — and a great white comforter. They thought the spotted shirt was the Great Manitou himself, the master of the alarming disease that swept them off in such vast numbers, and that the white comforter was the Manitou of the snow; that, if they could only secure and worship them, the small-pox would be banished, and abundant snows would drive the buffalo down from the mountains. The white man agreed to give them up, receiving in exchange several of their best horses; and for many years these two Manitous were carried in solemn procession to a hill consecrated to superstitious rites, laid reverently on the grass, and the great medicine-pipe (which is offered to the earth, the sun, and the water) was presented to them; the whole band singing, dancing, and howling around them.

Father Joseph treated the Indians altogether as children, and devised a system of object-teaching, making little images representing what they were to shun, and what to seek, to which he pointed in instructing them. He considered it a miracle, that they yielded their hearts to his teaching; but it seemed to me, that if the good priest's gentle ways and entire devotion to their welfare had produced no effect, it would have been as contradictory to all the laws of nature as any miracle could be. While instructing some savages from Puget Sound, he said the idea came into the mind of one of the priests, to represent by a ladder, which he made on paper, the various truths and mysteries of religion, in their chronological order. This proved vastly beneficial in instructing them. It was called the "Catholic ladder," and disseminated widely among the Indians; their progress in religion being measured by their knowledge of this ladder. At the same time that he sent the ladder among them, he sent also roots and seeds and agricultural tools. I could hardly repress a smile at seeing that he spoke with the same enthusiasm of their success with the beans and potatoes, as with the ladder. The truth is, that he had deeply at heart the good of these, his "wild children of the forest," as he always called them. It was quite touching to him, he said, to see how ready they were to believe that God took charge of earthly things as well as of heavenly.

One of his associates in the early missions was a Belgian priest, whose journal he showed us. He brought over, to aid in the work, six sisters of Notre Dame, in 1844. The vessel which brought them to the Pacific coast stopped at Valparaiso and Lima, to inquire how to enter the Columbia River. Not receiving any satisfactory information, they sailed north till they reached the forty-sixth degree of latitude. Then they explored for several days, and at length saw a sail coming out of what appeared to be the mouth of a river. They immediately sent an officer to find out from this vessel how to enter; but, as he did not return, they were obliged to approach alone the "vast and fearful mouth of the river," and soon found themselves in the terrible southern channel, into which, they were assured afterwards, no vessel had ever sailed before. The commander of the fort at Astoria had endeavored, by hoisting flags, by great signal-fires, and guns, to warn them of their danger. They saw the signals, but did not suspect their intention. They sailed two miles amidst fearful breakers. When at length they reached stiller water, a canoe approached them, containing an American man and some Clatsop Indians. The white man told them he would have come sooner to their aid, but the Indians refused to brave the danger; and said that he expected every moment to see the vessel dashed into a thousand pieces. The Indians, seeing it ride triumphantly over the dreadful bar, considered it under the special guidance of the Great Spirit, and greeted it with wild screams of delight. This was the introduction of the serene sisters to their field of labor. My idea of the sisters generally had been of pale, sad beings, whose most appropriate place was by the side of death-beds. These sisters of Notre Dame were brisk, energetic women, of lively temperaments. Finding the building which was preparing for them not yet provided with doors and windows, from the scarcity of mechanics, they themselves set about planing, glazing, and painting, to make every thing neat and comfortable. Wilkes, in his account of his exploring expedition, speaks regretfully of the poor appearance the Protestant missions presented, when compared with those of the Catholics; there being among the former an unthrifty, dilapidated look, and the Indians he saw there appeared to be employed only as servants.

The Catholics took pains to make all their ceremonies as imposing as circumstances would permit; making free use of musketry, bright colors, and singing, — things most attractive to an Indian, — remarking often, "Noise is essential to the Indian's enjoyment," and, "Without singing, the best instruction is of little value." They showed the Indians that they regarded the comfort and good of their bodies, as well as of their souls; giving them at Easter a great feast of potatoes, parsneps, turnips, beets, beans, and pease, to impress upon them the advantages of civilization, and taking pains that the requirements of religion should not interfere with the fishery or the chase. All the good customs and practices already established among them, they confirmed and approved, and found much to sympathize with in the Indians. The suavity and dignified simplicity of the chiefs particularly pleased them, and the relation of the chief to the people, — they consulting him in regard to every public or private undertaking, as when about to take a journey, or when entering upon marriage; he regulating the gathering of roots and berries, the hunting and fishing, and the division of spoils. The priests said of the chief, "He speaks calmly, but never in vain." They admired the self-control of the Indians, who never showed any impatience when misfortunes befell them; and said, that, the farther they penetrated into the wilderness, the better Indians they found. They were especially pleased with those about the sources of the Columbia, and said of their converts in that region, "If it be true that the prayer of him who possesses the innocence, the simplicity, and the faith of a child, pierces the clouds, then will the prayers of these dear children of the forest reach the ear of Heaven." They were interested in the different views of the future life held by the different tribes. To those who lived by woods and waters, heaven was a country of lakes, streams, and forests; but the Blackfoot heaven was of great sand-hills, stretching far and wide, abounding in game.

They devoted themselves with great zeal to reconciling hostile tribes, particularly the Blackfeet and Flat-heads. All the tribes feared the Blackfeet, especially that terrible sub-tribe called the "Blood Indians." The Snakes, too, were a common enemy to all the river-tribes. Father De Smet, the Belgian priest, with great intrepidity started for the Blackfoot country, although receiving numerous warnings of the risk he incurred. He encamped in the heart of their country. One of their chiefs sought him out, and took a fancy to the fearless old man at sight, embracing him in savage fashion, "rough but cordial." This chief was ornamented from head to foot with eagle-feathers, and dressed in blue as a mark of distinction. With this powerful friend, he immediately gained a footing among them. He conducted towards them with great wisdom and kindness, interfering as little as possible with their old customs. After he had made many converts among them, they asked him, on one of the great days of the Church, if he would like to see them manifest their joy in their own way,

— by painting, singing, and dancing; to which he gave courteous assent. The dance was performed wholly by women and children, although in the dress of warriors. Some of them carried arms, others only green boughs. All took part in it, from the toddling infant to the ancient grandam whose feeble limbs required the aid of a staff. They carried caskets of plumes, which nodded in harmony with their movements, and increased the graceful effect. There was also jingling of bells, and drums beaten by the men who surrounded them, and joined in the songs. To break the monotony, occasionally a sudden piercing scream was added. If the dance languished, haranguers and those most skilful in grimaces came to its aid. The movement consisted of a little jump, more or less lively according to the beat of the drum. It was danced on a beautiful green plain, under a cluster of pines. All the Indians climbed the trees, or sat round on their horses, to see it.

The missionaries secured some of their readiest converts among the Spokanes (children of the sun), who lived mostly on a great open plain. Instead of being crafty and reserved, like most of the tribes about them, they were free and genial. They welcomed the earliest explorers, and lived on friendly terms with the settlers. They were more susceptible to civilization and improvement than most of the other Indians.

Father De Smet was enthusiastic in his enjoyment of the forests and the mountains; speaking often of the "skyward palaces and holy towers" among the hills, "the immortal pine," the "rock-hung flower," the "fantastic grace of the winding rivers." The desert country through which he travelled, and of which we also saw something in coming to this place, he called "a little Arabia shut in by stern, Heaven-built walls of rock." In the narrow valleys at the foot of the Cascade Mountains, he found magnificent groves of rhododendrons, thousands of them together, fifteen or twenty feet high, — green arches formed underneath by their intertwined branches; above, bouquets of splendid flowers, shading from deepest crimson to pure white.

He mourned very much over the superstitions of the Indians; but said, nevertheless, that an attack of severe illness, which he suffered after one of his journeys, was no doubt sent as a punishment for his too carnal admiration of nature.

While we were talking with Father Joseph,

and looking over the journal, a messenger rode up to the door, and told him that *Tenas Marie* (Little Mary) was dying. The Indian agent, who stood by, said, "It is not much of a loss; she is a worthless creature." Father Joseph turned to him in a most dignified way, and said, "It is a human being;" and then to Christine, and asked if she would lend him a horse, she having a whole herd at command. Presently he started off for a whole night's ride. I thought, if I were Little Mary, after my bad life, when I must enter into account for it, I should be a good deal cheered and supported to see his kind eyes, and hear his firm voice directing me at the last.

The Cœurs d'Alêne (pointed hearts, or hearts of arrows — flint)[1] were so called from their determined resistance to having the white men come among them. They did not desire to have one of the Hudson Bay Company's posts upon their land, although the other tribes favored their establishment among them, wishing to barter their skins and obtain fire-arms; but said, that, if the white men saw their country, they would want to take it from them, it was so beautiful.

[1] To the Canadian *voyageur*, the word *alêne* (awl) meant any sharp-pointed instrument.

Father Joseph was their interpreter in the negotiations between them and the United-States Government. They attacked Col. Steptoe, while he was passing through their territory, because they had heard that the white men were going to build a road which would drive away the deer and the buffalo. It was explained to them, that, although this was so, other advantages would more than compensate for it. This was beyond their comprehension. To them, the advantages of civilization bore no comparison to the charm of their free, roving life. When the army officers entered the Cœur d'Alêne country, they declared that no conception of heaven could surpass the beauty of its exquisite lakes, embosomed in the forest. This tribe held firm against all propositions of the government to treat with them, until Donati's comet appeared in 1858; when, supposing it to be a great fiery broom sent to sweep them from the earth, they accepted a treaty.

The "Battle of Four Lakes" was fought in this country. An old man whom we met at the fort in Walla Walla, who saw this battle, gave us some account of it. The lakes are surrounded with rocks, covered with pine. Beyond them is a great rolling country of grassy hills. For about two miles, he said, this open ground was all alive with the wildest, most fantastic figures of mounted Indians, with painted horses, having eagle-feathers braided into their tails and manes; each Indian fighting separately on his own account. He described to us the appearance of the war chief as he rode to battle, his own head hidden by a wolf's head, with stiff, sharp ears standing erect, ornamented with bears' claws, and under it a circlet of feathers. From this head depended a long train of feathers that floated down his back; the loss of which would be the loss of his honor, and as great a disaster to him as, to a Chinaman, the loss of his cue. His war-horse was painted, as well as his own person, and also profusely decorated with feathers on head and tail. The Indians have such a fancy for feathers, that, in some of their medicine ceremonies, they smear their heads with a sticky substance, and cover them all over with swan's-down.

Lieut. Mullan's surveying expedition roused many of the tribes to desperation. Owhi, the Yakima chief, when urged to give up his land, —or, what amounted to the same thing, to allow free passage to the surveying-party and the road-makers, — argued that he could not give away the home of his people; saying, "It is not mine to give. The Great Spirit has *measured* it to my people." Not being successful in his arguments, he organized the outbreak of the following winter. The army destroyed the *caches* filled with dried berries, and the pressed cake which the Indians prepare from roots for their winter food, many lodges filled with grain, and hundreds of horses; the officers mentioning in their report, that it would insure the Indians a winter of great suffering, and concluding in these words: "Seldom has an expedition been undertaken, the recollection of which is invested with so much that is agreeable, as that against the Northern Indians."

# VI.

**Colville to Seattle. — "Red." — "Ferrins." — "Broke Miners." — A Rare Fellow-Traveller. — The Bell-Mare. — Pelouse Fall. — Red-fox Road. — Early Californians. — Frying-pan Incense. — Dragon-flies. — Death of the Chief Seattle.**

SEATTLE, Aug. 23, 1866.

WE were detained at Fort Colville several days longer than we desired, seeking an opportunity to get back to the Columbia River, by some chance wagon going down from the mines, or from some of the supply-stations in the upper country. In our expedition on the "Forty-nine," we had seen a great many miners, and, among them, one horrid character, with a flaming beard, who was known by every one as "Red." He had been mining in the snow mountains, far up in British Columbia, and joined us to go down on the steamer to Colville. He was terribly rough and tattered-looking. The mining-season in those northern mountains is so short, that he said he was going back to winter at the mines, so as to be on the spot for work in the spring, and that he should take up about forty gallons of grease to keep himself warm through the winter.

He and his companions told great stories about their rough times in the mountains. Some of them mentioned having been reduced to the extremity of living on "ferrins" when all other food had failed. These accounts were generally received, by the rest of the miners, with great outbursts of laughter. That appeared to be their customary way of regarding all their misfortunes, — at least, in the retrospect. We wondered what the "ferrins" could be. Nobody seemed to resort to them, except in the direst need. Upon inquiry, we found out that they were *boiled ferns.* I have always noticed that even insects of all kinds pass by ferns. I suspect that even the hungriest man would find them rather unsatisfying, but this light diet seemed to have kept them in the most jovial spirits.

R. was rather averse to travelling in such company, and always presented "Red" to me as the typical miner, when opportunities offered for our getting down from Colville with a party from the mines. Finally I persuaded him to accept either "Buffalo Bill," who offered to take us by ourselves, or an Irishman who insisted upon having a few miners with him. I think he was rather prejudiced against the former, on account of his name; and we therefore made an agreement with the latter, to take us, with only two miners, instead of ten as he at first desired, that R. should see them before we started, and that we should have the wagon to ourselves at night. As it happened, we left in haste, and did not see the miners until they leaped from the wagon, and began to assist in putting in our baggage. That was not an occasion, of course, for criticising them. Besides that, I saw, when I first looked at them, that they were rather harder to read than most people I had met; and I could not in a minute tell what to make of them. Our wagoner said they were "broke miners." I did not know exactly what that meant, but thought they might be very desperate characters, made more so by special circumstances. One of them looked like a brigand, with his dark hair and eyes. But I didn't mind; for I was tired of travelling about, and anxious to get home. I thought I would sleep most of the way down; so I put back my head, and shut my eyes. Presently the dark man began to talk with R., in a musical voice, about the soft Spanish names of places in California; and I could not sleep much. Then he spoke of the primitive forms in which minerals crystallized, the five-sided columns of volcanic rock, and the little cubes of gold. I could make no pretence at sleep any longer; I had to open my eyes; and once in a while I asked a question or two, although I would not show much interest, and determined not to become at all acquainted with him, because we were necessarily to be very intimate, travelling all day together, and camping together at night. But I watched him a great deal, and listened to his conversation upon many subjects. I think, that not only on this journey, but in all the time since we came to this coast, we have not enjoyed any thing else so much. He had uncommon powers of expression, and of thought and feeling too, and took great interest in every thing. He had even a little tin box of insects. He showed us the native grains, wild rice, etc., the footprints of animals, the craters of old volcanoes, and called us to listen to the wild doves at night, and the cry of the loon and the curlew.

We travelled in a large freight-wagon, drawn by four mules. A pretty little "bell-mare" followed the wagon. At night she was tied out on the plain; and the mules were turned loose to feed, and were kept from wandering far away by the tinkle of the bell hung on her neck. We slept on beautiful flowering grass, which our wagoner procured for us on the way. When he tied great bunches of it on the front of the wagon, to feed the animals when they came to a barren place, it looked as if we were preparing to take part in some floral procession. The first night, we camped in the midst of the pine-trees. When I woke in the night, and looked round me, the row of dark figures on either side seemed like the genii in "The Arabian Nights," that used to guard sleeping princesses.

Besides the knowledge which our fellow-traveller possessed of the country through which we were passing, which made him a valuable companion to us then, his general enthusiasm would have made him interesting anywhere. I remember a little incident at one of our noon stopping-places, which we thought was very much to his credit. He always hastened to make a fire as soon as we stopped. It was rather hard to find good places, sheltered from the wind, where it would burn, and which would furnish us, too, with a little shade. On this occasion there was a magnificent tree very near us. We were passing out of the region of trees, so it was a particularly welcome sight.

He started the fire close to it. It happened to be too near; the pitch caught fire, and presently the trunk was encircled with flame. He was desperate to think that he should have been guilty of an act of "such wanton destructiveness," as he called it, — especially as it was the last fine tree on the road. He abandoned all idea of dinner, and did nothing through that fiery noon, when we could hardly stir from the shade, — which we found farther off, — but rush between the stream near by and the tree, with his little camp-kettle of water, to try to save it. He looked back with such a grateful face, as we left the spot, to see that the flames were smothered. There was something like a child about him; that is, an uncommon freedom from the wickedness that seems to belong to most men, certainly the class he is in the habit of associating with. I doubt if there is one of the men we saw on the "Forty-nine" who would not have been delighted to burn that tree down; and how few of them would have thought, as he did, to put the little pieces of wood that we had to spare, where fuel was scarce, into the road, so that "some other old fellow, who might chance to come along, might see them and use them"!

He told us one beautiful story about miners,

though, in connection with the loss of the "Central America." He had a friend on board among the passengers, who were almost all miners going home. When they all expected to perish with the vessel, a Danish brig hove in sight, and came to the rescue. But the passengers could not all be transferred to her. They filled the ship's boats with their wives and their treasure, and sent them off; and the great body of them went down with a cheer and a shout, as the vessel keeled over.

The event of special interest, in our journey home, was our visit to the Pelouse Fall. We had heard that there was a magnificent fall on the Pelouse, twelve miles by trail from the wagon-road, which we were very desirous of seeing; but no one could give us exact directions for finding it. Our friend the miner wanted very much to see it also; and as he seemed to have quite an instinct for finding his way, by rock formations and other natural features of the country, we ventured to attempt it with him. The little bell-mare, which was a *cayuse* (Indian) horse, was offered for my use, and an old Spanish wooden saddle placed upon her back. I had no bridle; but I had been presented at the fort with a *hackama* (a buffalo-hair rope), such as the Indians use with their horses. This was attached to the head of the horse, so that the miner could lead her. My saddle had an arrangement in front by which to attach the lasso, in catching animals. The miner said that just the same pattern was still in use in Andalusia and other Spanish provinces. I felt as if I were starting on quite a new career. When he lifted me on to the horse, he said, "How light you are!" It was because every care had dropped off from me.

We rode over the wildest desert country, with great black walls of rock, and wonderful cañons, with perpendicular sides, extending far down into the earth. Mr. Bowles, in his book, "Across the Continent," says he cannot compare any thing else to the exhilaration of the air of the upland plains; neither sea nor mountain air can equal it. The extreme heat, too, seemed to intensify every thing in us, even our power of enjoyment, notwithstanding the discomfort of it. The thermometer marked 117° in the shade. I felt as if I had never before known what breezes and shadows and streams were. Just as we had reached the last limit of possible endurance, the shadow of some great wall of rock would fall upon us, or a little breeze spring up, or we would find the land descending to the bed of a stream. At length our miner, who had been for the last part of the way looking and listening with the closest attention, struck almost directly to the spot, hardly a step astray. It was all below the surface of the earth, so that hardly any sound rose above; and there was no sign of any path to it, not a tree, nor shrub, nor blade of grass near, but an amphitheatre of rock, and the beautiful white river, in its leap into the cañon falling a hundred and ninety feet. The cliffs and jagged pinnacles of basaltic rock around it were several hundred feet high. It looked like a great white bridal veil. It was made up of myriads of snowy sheaves, sometimes with the faintest amethyst tint. It shattered itself wholly into spray before it struck the water below, — that is, the outer circumference of it, — and the inner part was all that made any sound.

The miner looked upon it with perfect rapture. He said to me, "It is a rare pleasure to travel with any one who enjoys any thing of this kind." I felt it so too.

His striking directly at the spot, after many miles of travel, without any landmarks, reminded me of the experience of Ross, the Hudson Bay trader, when he travelled from Fort Okanagan on foot, two hundred miles to the coast, taking with him an Indian, who told him they would go by the Red Fox road; that is, the road by which Red Fox the chief and his men used to go. After they had travelled a long distance over a pathless country, without any sign of a trail, or climbed along the rocky banks of streams, he asked his guide when they would reach the Red Fox road. "This is it, you are on," was the reply. "Where?" eagerly inquired Ross: "I see no road here, not even so much as a rabbit could walk on." — "Oh, there is no road," answered the Indian: "this is the place where they used to pass."

At another time, when he was travelling with an Indian guide, who was accompanied by some of his relatives, the latter were left at a place called Friendly Lake, and were to be called for on their return. They went on to their journey's end, and on their way back, some days after, stopped at the place; but no sign of the relatives appeared. The guide, however, searched about diligently, and presently pointed to a small stick, stuck up in the ground, with a little notch in it. He said, "They are there," pointing in the direction in which the stick slanted, — "one day's journey off." Exactly there they were found.

There was a kind of generosity about this

"broke miner," that made us ready to forgive a great deal in him. No doubt there would have been a great deal to forgive if we had known him more. He was, very likely, in the habit of drinking and gambling, like the others that we saw. I know he was a terrible tobacco chewer and smoker. He has been seventeen years on the Pacific side of the continent, came out as a "forty-niner," has travelled a great deal, and taken notes of all he has seen, and said he thought of making use of them some time, if his employments would ever admit of it. I think he is the best fitted to describe the country, of all the persons I have met.

He gave us quite a vivid idea of the semi-barbarous life of the California pioneers, and of the intense desire they sometimes felt for a glimpse of their homes, their wives, and children. I remembered Starr King's saying that women and children had been more highly appreciated in California ever since, on account of their scarcity during the first few years. I rather think the sentiment of the miners was somewhat intensified by the extreme difficulty they found in doing women's work. One of them, now an eminent physician, pricked and scarred his fingers in the most distressing manner, in attempting to sew on his buttons, and patch the rents in his garments. Another member of the camp, who was afterwards governor of the State, won his first laurels as a cook, by the happy discovery, that, by combining an acid with the alkali used in the making of their bread, the result was vastly more satisfactory than where the alkali alone was used. In crossing the plains, they had used the alkali water found there for this purpose.

A travelling theatrical company, who presented themselves with the announcement that they would perform a drama entitled "The Wife," met with unbounded appreciation. Carpenters were employed at sixteen dollars a day to prepare for its presentation. This was the first play ever acted in San Francisco. The company were encouraged to remain, and give other performances; but, as there was only one lady actor, every play had to be altered to conform to this condition of things.

The most tempting advertisement a restaurant could offer was, "potatoes at every meal." Those who indulged in fresh eggs did so at an expense of one dollar per egg.

When the signal from Telegraph Hill announced the arrival of the monthly mail-steamer, there was a general rush for the post-office; and a long line was formed, reaching from the office out to the tents in the chapparal. The building was a small one, and the facilities for assorting and delivering the mail so limited, that many hours were consumed in the work. Large prices were often paid for places near the head of the line; and some of the more eager ones would wrap their blankets around them, and stand all night waiting, in order to get an early chance.

Thus, with endless stories and anecdotes, accounts of his adventures as a miner and explorer, and descriptions of the new and wonderful places he had visited, and the curious people he had met, our fellow-traveller beguiled the tediousness of the journey, and continually entertained us.

As we approached Walla Walla, we made our last camp at the Touchet, a lovely stream. I woke in the morning feeling as if some terrible misfortune had befallen us. I could not tell what, until I was fully roused, and found it could be nothing else than that we must sleep in a bed that night.

We left our miner in Walla Walla, to get work, I think, as a machinist. My acquaintance with him was a lesson to me, never to judge any one by appearance or occupation. We met afterwards some little, common-looking men, who had been so successful at the mines that they could hardly carry their sacks of gold-dust, which made hard white ridges in their hands. They had fifteen thousand dollars or more apiece. I thought, how unequally and unwisely Fate distributes her gifts; but then, as Mrs. S. said when there was such a rush for the garments brought on board the steamer for us at Panama, after our shipwreck, "Let those have them who can least gracefully support the want of them."

Among the miners of the upper country, who had not seen a white woman for a year, I received such honors, that I am afraid I should have had a very mistaken impression of my importance if I had lived long among them. At every stopping-place they made little fires in their frying-pans, and set them around me, to keep off the mosquitoes, while I took my meal. As the columns of smoke rose about me, I felt like a heathen goddess, to whom incense was being offered. The mosquitoes were terrible; but we found our compensation for them in the journey homeward. I remember the entomology used to call the dragon-fly the "mosquito-hawk;" and such dragon-flies I never before saw as we met with near the rivers, especially at the Pelouse. There seemed to be a festival of them there, and one kind of such a green as I believe never was seen before on earth, — so exquisite a shade, and so vivid. There were also burnished silver and gold ones, and every beautiful variety of spotting and marking. A little Indian boy appeared there, dressed in feathers, with a hawk on his wrist, — a wild, spirited-looking little creature.

On Sunday we reached Olympia, and saw the waters of the Sound, and the old headlands again. I had no idea it could look so homelike; and when the mountain range began to reveal itself from the mist, I felt as if nothing we had seen while we were gone had been more beautiful, more really impressive, than what we could look at any day from our own kitchen-door.

As we approached Seattle, we began to gather up the news. It is very much more of an event to get back, when you have had no newspapers, and only the rarest communication of any kind, while you have been gone.

Seattle, the old chief, had died. When he was near his end, he sent word over to the nearest settlement, that he wished Capt. Meigs, the owner of the great sawmill at Port Madison, to come when he was dead, and take him by the hand, and bid him farewell.

We learned that the beautiful Port Angeles

was to be abandoned, — Congress having decided to remove the custom-house to Port Townsend, — and that no vessels would go in there. It seemed like leaving Andromeda on her rock. We are going down to make a farewell visit.

# VII.

Port Angeles Village and the Indian Ranch. — A "Ship's *Klootchman*." — Indian *Muck-a-Muck*. — Disposition of an Old Indian Woman. — A Windy Trip to Victoria. — The Black *Tamáhnous*. — McDonald's in the Wilderness. — The Wild Cowlitz. — Up the River during a Flood. — Indian Boatmen. — Birch-bark and Cedar Canoes.

EDIZ HOOK, Oct. 21, 1866.

WE are making a visit at the end of Ediz Hook. No one lives here now but the light-keepers. When we feel the need of company, we look across to the village of Port Angeles and the Indian ranch. It is very striking to see how much more picturesque one is than the other, in the distance. In the village, all the trees have been cut down ; but the lodges of the Indians stand in the midst of a maple grove, and in this Indian-summer weather there is always a lovely haze about it, bright leaves, and blue beams of mist across the trees. Living so much out of doors as they do, and in open lodges, their little fires are often seen, giving their ranch a hospitable look, and making the appearance of the village very uninviting in comparison.

Oct. 26, 1866.

We have had a great storm; and last night, about dark, a white figure of a woman appeared in the water, rising and falling, outside the breakers. Some Indians went out in their canoes, and took her in to the shore. One of them came to tell us about it. A "ship's *klootchman*" (wife or woman), he said it was, and a "*hyas* [big] ship" must have gone down. It was the figure-head of a vessel. The next morning, I saw that the Indians had set it up on the sand, with great wings — which they made of broken pieces of spars — at the sides. It was the large, handsome figure of a woman, twice life-size. They seemed to regard it as a kind of goddess; and I felt half inclined to, myself, she looked out so serenely at the water. I sat down by her side, thinking about what had probably happened, to try to get her calm way of regarding it. A sloop was sent over from the custom-house, to take it across the bay for identification; but that proved impracticable. The captain said that he knew the work, — it was English carving. Soon after, a vessel came in, having lost her figure-head. The men on board said that a strange ship ran into her in the night, and immediately disappeared. They supposed she was much injured, as they afterwards saw a deck-load of lumber floating, which they thought had come from her. They said it might be the "Radama," bound for China.

OCT 29, 1866.

To-day, when we were coasting along the shore, we saw Yeomans preparing his canoe for a long excursion. It was lined with mats. In the middle were two of the baskets the Indians weave from roots, filled with red salmon-spawn. Against them lay a gray duck, with snowy breast; then, deer-meat, and various kinds of fishes. Over the whole he had laid great green leaves that looked like the leaves of the tulip-tree. The narrow end of the canoe was filled with purple sea-urchins, all alive, and of the most vivid color. I took one up, and asked him if they were good to eat. He said, "Indian *muck-a-muck*, not for Bostons" (whites). His arrangements looked a great deal more picturesque than our preparations for picnics.

The light-keeper at Ediz Hook told us to-day that he had exhumed an old Indian woman, whom some of her tribe had buried alive, or, rather, wrapped up and laid away in one of the little wooden huts in their graveyard, according to their custom of disposing of the dead. They had apparently become tired of the care of her, and concluded to anticipate her natural exit from the world by this summary disposition of her. Mr. S. heard her cries, and went to the rescue. He restored her to the tribe, with a reprimand for their barbarity, and told them the Bostons would not tolerate such *mesahchie* (outrageous) proceedings.

PORT ANGELES, Oct. 31, 1866.

We made a spirited voyage to Victoria, across the Straits of Fuca. There had been a very severe storm, which we thought was over; but it had a wild ending, after we were on our way, and beyond the possibility of return. We saw the California steamer, ocean-bound, putting back to port. Our only course was to hasten on. The spray was all rainbows, and there were low rainbows in the sky, — incomprehensible rainbows above and below, — and the strongest wind that ever blew. It was all too wonderful for us to be afraid: it was like a new existence; as if we had cast off all connection with the old one, and were spirits only. We flew past the high shores, and looked up at the happy, homelike houses, with a strange feeling of isolation and independence of all earthly ties.

I staid on deck till every man had gone in, feeling that I belonged wholly to wind and wave, borne on like a bird. But the captain came and took me in, lest I should be swept from the deck. When we reached Victoria, great wooden signs were being blown off the stores, and knocking down the people in the streets. This is certainly the home of the winds.

Nov. 20, 1866.

To-day we met on the beach Tleyuk (Spark of Fire), a young Indian with whom we had become acquainted. Instead of the pleasant "*Klahowya*" (How do you do?), with which he was accustomed to greet us, he took no notice of us whatever. On coming nearer, we saw hideous streaks of black paint on his face, and on various parts of his body, and inquired what they meant. His English was very meagre; but he gave us to understand, in a few hoarse gutturals, that they meant hostility and danger to any one that interfered with him. We noticed afterwards other Indians, with dark, threatening looks, and daubed with black paint, gathering from different directions. The old light-keeper was launching his boat to cross over to the spit, and we turned to him for an explanation. He warned us to keep away from the Indians, as this was the time of the "Black *Tamáhnous*," when they call up all their hostility to the whites. He pointed to some Indian children, who had a white elk-horn, like a dwarf white man, stuck up in the sand to throw stones at. I had noticed for the last few days, when I met them in the narrow paths in the woods, that they stopped straight before me, obliging me to turn aside for them.

We saw them withdraw to an old lodge in the woods, as if to hold a secret council. We did not feel much concerned as to the result of it for ourselves, as we held such friendly relations to Yeomans, the old chief, and had always given the Indians all the sea-bread they wanted, — that being the one article of our food that they seemed most to appreciate. As it proved, it was a mere thunder-cloud, dissipated after a few growls.

**McDonald's, Dec. 18, 1866.**

Not knowing the name of the nearest town, I date this from McDonald's, that having been our last stopping-place. It is on the stage-route between Columbia River and Puget Sound, and a place worth remembering. I wish I could give an idea of its cheeriness, especially after travelling a fortnight in the rain, as we have done. At this season of the year, every thing is deluged; and the roads, full of deep mud-holes and formidable stumps, are now at their worst. The heavy wagons move slowly and laboriously forward, sometimes getting so deep in the mire that it is almost impossible to extricate them, and at times impeded by fallen trees, which the driver has to cut away. They are poorly protected against the searching rains, and for the last two days we have been drenched.

When we caught the first glimpse of the red light in the distance, we felt very much inclined to appreciate any thing approaching comfort, tired and dripping as we were; but what our happy Fates had in store for us, we never for a moment imagined. We had hardly entered the house before we felt that it was no common place. The fireplace was like a great cavern, full of immense logs and blazing bark. It lighted up a most hospitable room. From a beam in the low ceiling, hung a great branch of apples. I counted twenty-three bright red and yellow apples shining out from it.

Two stages meet here, and the main business at this time of the year is drying the passengers sufficiently for them to proceed on their way the next day. The host and his family stood round the fire, handling and turning the wet garments with unbounded good-nature and patience. The stage-drivers cracked jokes and told stories. A spirit of perfect equality prevailed, and a readiness to take every thing in the best possible part. The family are Scotch, — hard-working people; but they have not worked so hard as to rub all the bloom off their lives, as so many people have that we have seen.

When supper was announced, another surprise awaited us. Instead of the unvarying round of fried meat and clammy pie with which we had hitherto been welcomed, we were refreshed with a dish of boiled meat, a corn-starch pudding, and stewed plums. Why some other dweller in the wilderness could not have introduced a little variety into his bill of fare, we could never conceive. It seemed a real inspiration in McDonald, to send to California or Oregon for a little dried fruit and some papers of corn-starch. He gave us, too, what was even more delightful than his wholesome food, — a little glimpse of his home-life. To a tired traveller, what could be more refreshing than a sight of somebody's home? Generally, at whatever place we stopped, we saw only the "menfolks;" the family, often half-breed, being huddled away in the rear. Here, in the room in which the guests were received, lay the smiling baby in its old-fashioned cradle. Two blithe little girls danced in and out, and the old grandfather sat holding a white-haired boy. When dinner was over, the great business of drying the clothes was resumed by the travellers and the family; and we held our wrappings by the fire, and turned them about, until we became so drowsy that we lost all sense of responsibility. We found, the next morning, that our host sat up and finished all that were left undone. He had become so accustomed to this kind of work, that he did not seem to consider it was any thing extra, or that it entitled him to any further compensation than the usual one for a meal and a night's lodging. When we offered something more, he pointed to a little box nailed up beside the door, over which was a notice that any one who wished might contribute something for a school which the Sisters were attempting to open for the children of that neighborhood. Being Scotch people, I could hardly believe they were Catholics; but found upon inquiry that their views were so liberal as to enable them to appreciate the advantages of education, by whomsoever offered. I was quite touched by McDonald's little contribution to civilization, in the midst of the wilderness. As I looked back, in leaving, at the great trees and the exquisitely curved slope of his little clearing, I felt that in the small log house was something worthy of the fine surroundings.

OLYMPIA, Dec. 23, 1866.

When we reached Cowlitz Landing, we found the river quite different in character from what we had known it before. It had risen many feet above its ordinary level, and was still rising, and had become a wide, fierce, and rushing stream, bearing on its surface great trees and fragments of wrecked buildings, swiftly sailing down to the Columbia. How serenely we descended the river last year, floating along at sunset, admiring the lovely valley and the hills, reaching over the side of the canoe, and soaking our biscuits in the glacier-water, without once thinking of the vicissitudes to which we were liable from its mountain origin!

The little steamer that recently had begun to compete with the Indian canoes in the traffic of the river, and the carrying of passengers, did not dare to attempt to ascend it. Navigation was not to be thought of by ordinary boats, or by white men, and was possible only by canoes in the most trusty hands. No land-conveyance could be had at this point. We were told that we might take the stream, by those familiar with it, if we could find good Indians willing to go with us. One called "Shorty" was brought forward to negotiate with us. He has the same dwarfed appearance I have noticed in the old women, and that strange, Egyptian-looking face and air. It would be impossible for any one to tell, by his appearance, whether he personally were old or young; but the ancientness of the type is deeply impressed upon him. If half-civilized Indians had been offered, or those that had had much intercourse with the whites, I should have hesitated more to trust them; but he was such a pure Indian, it seemed as if he were as safe as any wild creature. Whether he would extend any help, in emergencies, to his clumsy civilized passengers, was a more doubtful question. However, as the alternative was to wait indefinitely, and the character of the stopping-places, as a rule, drives one to desperate measures, we confided ourselves to his hands, and embarked with him and his assistant, a fine athletic young Indian.

We fixed our eyes intently upon him, as if studying our fates. He was perfectly imperturbable, and steered only, the other poling the canoe along the edge of the stream, and grasping the overhanging trees to pull it along, using the paddle only when these means were not available. His work required unceasing vigilance and activity, and was so hard that it would have exhausted any ordinary man in a few hours; but he kept on from early morning till dark. Always in the most difficult places, or if his energy seemed to flag in the least, Shorty would call out to him, in the most animated manner, mentioning a canoe, a hammock, and a *hyas closhe* (very nice) *klootchman;* at which the young man would laugh with delight, and start anew. I considered it was probably his stock in life, the prospect of an establishment, which was presented to rouse and cheer him on. Shorty had been recommended to us as one of the best hands on the river. I began to see that it was for his power of inspiring others, as well as for his extreme vigilance in keeping out of the eddies, and avoiding the drift in crossing the river, to be caught in which would have been destruction. We crossed several times, to secure advantages which his quick eye perceived. I noticed that whenever he pointed out any particular branch on the shore to be seized, how certain the other was to strike it at once. With white men, how much blundering and missing there would have been!

I never felt before, so strongly, how many vices attend civilization, which it seems as if men might just as well be free from, as when I compared these Indians with the common white people about us, — the stage-drivers, mill-men, and others, — with no smoking nor drinking nor tobacco-chewing, and so strong and graceful, and sure in their aim, that no gymnast I have ever seen could compare with them. The ingenious ways in which they helped themselves along in places where any boat of ours would have been immediately overturned, converting obstacles often into helps, were fascinating to study. As night came on, I began to wish that their consciences were a little more developed, or, rather, that they had a little more sense of responsibility with regard to us. The safety of their passengers is no burden whatever on the minds of the Indians. Their spirits seem to rise with danger. They know that they could very well save themselves in an emergency, and I believe they prefer that white people should be drowned. I could only look into the imperturbable faces of our boatmen, and wonder where we were to spend the night. Finally, with a terrible whirl, which I felt at the time must be our last, they entered a white foaming slough (a branch of the river), and drew up on the bank. They announced to us then that we were to walk a mile through the woods, to a house. I think no white man, even the most surly of our drivers, would have asked us to do that, — in perfect blackness, the trees wet and dripping, — but would have managed to bring us to some inhabited place. They started off at a rapid gait, and we followed. We could not see their forms; but one carried something white in his hand, which we faintly discerned in the darkness, which served as our guide. They sang and shouted, and sounded their horn, all the way. I supposed it was to keep off bad spirits, but the next day we heard that in those woods bears and panthers were sometimes found. At length a light appeared. We felt cheered; but when we approached it, two furious dogs rushed out at us. They were immediately followed by their master, who took us in. After consultation with him, we concluded to abandon our Indians, as he said he could take us, on the following day, through the woods to the next stopping-place, with his ox-team. The quiet comfort of being transported by oxen was something not to be resisted, after having our nerves so racked. We felt an immense satisfaction in coming again upon our own kind, even if it were only in an old log cabin, where the children were taken out of their bed to put us in.

We have seen no bark canoes here; they are all of cedar. No doubt there is good canoe-birch on the river-banks, but something more durable is needed. The North-west Fur Company, in early days, sent out a cargo of birch from Montreal to London, to be shipped from there round Cape Horn to the north-west coast of America, to be made into canoes for their men to navigate the Columbia and its branches; in direst ignorance of the requirements of the country, as well as of its productions.

# VIII.

Voyage to San Francisco. — Fog-bound. — Port Angeles. — Passing Cape Flattery in a Storm. — Off Shore. — The "Brontes." — The Captain and his Men. — A Fair Wind. — San Francisco Bar. — The City at Night. — Voyage to Astoria. — Crescent City. — Iron-bound Coast. — Mount St. Helen's. — Mount Hood. — Cowlitz Valley and its Floods. — Monticello.

SAN FRANCISCO, Feb. 20, 1867.

WE are here at last, contrary to all our expectations for the last ten days. We left Puget Sound at short notice, taking passage on the first lumber-vessel that was available, with many misgivings, as she was a dilapidated-looking craft. We went on board at Port Madison, about dusk, — a dreary time to start on a sea-voyage, but we had to accommodate ourselves to the tide. The cabin was such a forlorn-looking place, that I was half tempted to give it up at the last; when I saw, sitting beside the rusty, empty stove, a small gray-and-white cat, purring, and rubbing her paws in the most cheery manner. The contrast between the great, cold, tossing ocean, and that little comfortable creature, making the best of her circumstances, so impressed me, that I felt ashamed to shrink from the voyage, if she was willing to undertake it. So I unpacked my bundles, and settled down for a rough time. There were only two of us as passengers, lumber-vessels not making it a part of their business to provide specially for their accommodation.

The sky looked threatening when we started; and the captain said, if he thought there was a storm beginning, he would not try to go on. But as we got out into the Straits of Fuca, the next day, a little barque, the "Crimea," came up, and said she had been a week trying to get out of the straits, and thought the steady southwest wind, which had prevented her, could not blow much longer. We continued beating down towards the ocean, and in the afternoon a dense fog shut us in. The last thing we saw was an ocean-steamer, putting back to Victoria for shelter. Our captain said his vessel drew too much water for Victoria Harbor, and the entrance was too crooked to attempt; but, if he could find Port Angeles, he would put in there. A gleam of sunshine shot through the fog, and showed us the entrance; and we steered triumphantly for that refuge. Two other vessels had anchored there. But just as we were about rounding the point to enter, and were congratulating ourselves on the quiet night we hoped to spend under the shelter of the mountains, the captain spied a sail going on towards the ocean. He put his vessel right about, determined to face whatever risks any other man would. But the vessel seemed unwilling to go. All that night, and the next day, and the next night, we rode to and fro in the straits, unable to get out.

Passing Cape Flattery is the great event of the voyage. It is always rough there, from the peculiar conformation of the land, and the conflict of the waters from the Gulf of Georgia, and other inlets, with the ocean-tides. Our captain had been sailing on this route for fifteen years, but said he had never seen a worse sea than we encountered. We asked him if he did not consider the Pacific a more uncertain ocean than the Atlantic. At first he said "Yes;" then, "No, it is pretty certain to be bad here at all times." What could Magellan's idea have been in so naming it? He, however, sailed in more southern latitudes, where it may be stiller. We expected to sail *on* the water; but our vessel drove *through* it, just as I have seen the snow-plough drive through the great drifts after a storm. Going to sea on a steamer gives one no idea of the winds and waves, — the real life of the ocean, — compared to what we get on a sailing-vessel. Every time we tried to round the point, great walls of waves advanced against us, — so powerful and defiant-looking, that I could only shut my eyes when they drew near. It did not seem as if I made a prayer, but as if I were myself a prayer, only a winged cry. I knew then what it must be to die. I felt that I fled from the angry sea, and reached, in an instant, serene heights above the storm.

Finally, as the result of all these desperate efforts, in which we recognized no gain, the captain announced that we had made the point, but we could get no farther until the wind changed; and, while we still felt the fury of the contrary sea, it was hard to recognize that we had much to be grateful for. We saw one beautiful sight, though, — a vessel going home, helped by the wind that hindered us. It was at night; and the light struck up on her dark sails, and made them look like wings, as she flew over the water. What bliss it seemed, to be nearing home, and all things in her favor!

I could hear all about us a heavy sound like surf on the shore, which was quite incomprehensible, as we were so far from land. But the water drove us from the deck. The vessel plunged head foremost, and reeled from side to side, with terrible groaning and straining. If we attempted to move, we were violently thrown in one direction or another; and finally found that all we could do was to lie still on the cabin-floor, holding fast to any thing stationary that we could reach. We could hear the water sweeping over the deck above us, and several times it poured down in great sheets upon us. We ventured to ask the captain what he was attempting to do. "Get out to sea," he said, "out of the reach of storms." That is brave sailing, I thought, though I would not have gone if I could have helped it. We struggled on in this way for a day and a night, and then he said we were beyond the region of storms from land. I am afraid I should, if left to myself, linger always with the faint-hearted mariners who hug the shore, notwithstanding this great experience of finding our safety by steering boldly off from every thing wherein we had before considered our only security lay. After this, I performed every day the great exploit of climbing to the deck, and looking out at the waste of water. I saw only one poor old vessel, pitching and reeling like a drunken man. I wondered if we could look so to her. She was always half-seas-over. I came to the conclusion it was best not to watch her, but it was hard to keep my eyes off of her. She was our companion all the way down, always re-appearing after every gale we weathered, though often far behind. I remember, just as we were fairly under way, hearing a man sing out, "There's the old 'Brontes' coming out of the straits." My associations with the name were gloomy in the extreme.

When the wind and sea were at their worst, considering the extremity, we felt called upon to offer some advice to the captain, and suggested that, under such circumstances, it might be advisable to travel under bare poles; but that, he assured us, was only resorted to when a man's voice could not possibly be heard in giving orders.

The captain was quite a study to us. On shore he presented the most ordinary appearance. When we had been out two or three days, I noticed some one I had not seen before on deck, and thought to myself, "That is an apparition for a time of danger, — a man as resolute as the sea itself, so stern and gray-looking." I was quite bewildered, for I thought I must certainly before that have seen every one on board. It proved to be the captain in his storm-clothes. One of the sailors was a Russian serf, running away, as he said, from the Czar of Russia, not wholly believing in the safety of the serfs. He had shipped as a competent seaman; but when he was sent up to the top of the mizzen-mast, to fix the halliards for a signal, he stopped in the most perilous place, and announced that he could not go any farther. It seems that every man on board was a stranger to the captain. It filled us with anxiety to think how much depended on that one man. One night there was an alarm of "A man overboard!" If it had been the captain, how aimlessly we should have drifted on! I liked to listen, when we were below, to hear the men hoisting the sails, and shouting together. It sounded as if they were managing horses, now restraining them, and now cheering them on. When the captain put his hand on the helm, we could always tell below. There was as much difference as in driving. In the midst of the wildest plunging, he would suddenly quiet it by putting the vessel in some other position, just as he would have held in a rearing horse.

Two or three times, when there was a little lull, I went on deck; and the air was as balmy as from a garden. What can it mean, this fragrance of fresh flowers in the midst of the sea?

Some virtues, I think, are admirably cultivated at sea. Night after night, as we lay there, I said to the captain, "What is the meaning of those clouds?" or "that dull red sky?" And he answered so composedly, "It's going to be squally," that I admired his patience; but it wore upon us very much.

At length, one night, as I lay looking up through our little skylight, at the flapping of the great white spanker-sheet, — my special enemy and dread, because the captain would keep it up when I thought it unsafe, it seemed such a lawless thing, and so ready to overturn us every time it shifted, — a great cheerful star looked in. It meant that all trouble was over. One after another followed it. I could not speak, I was so glad. I could only look at them, and feel that our safety was assured. The wind had changed. I appreciated the delight of Ulysses in "the fresh North Spirit" Calypso gave him "to guide him o'er the sea," — the rest of our voyage was so exhilarating.

We had one more special risk only, — crossing the bar of San Francisco Bay. The captain said, if he reached it at night, he expected to wait until daylight to enter; but I knew that his ambitious spirit would never let him, if it were possible to get over. About three o'clock in the morning, I heard a new sound in the water, like the rippling of billows, as if it were shallow. I hastened upon deck, and found that we were apparently on the bar. The captain and the mate differed about the sounding. Immediately after, I heard the captain tell a man to run down and see what time it was; and, upon learning the hour, heard him exclaim, in the deepest satisfaction, "Flood-tide, sure! Well, we had a chance!" I felt as if we had had a series of chances from the time we left Port Angeles Harbor, to the running in without a pilot, and drifting, as we did, into the revenue-cutter, just as we anchored. We had a beautiful entrance, though. It is a long passage, an hour or two after crossing the bar. San Francisco lay in misty light before us, like one of the great bright nebulæ we used to look at in Hercules, or the sword-handle of Perseus. It is splendidly lighted. As we drew nearer, there seemed to be troops of stars over all the hills.

**Astoria, Ore., Oct. 17, 1868.**

In making the voyage from San Francisco, I could hardly go on deck at all, until the last day; but, lying and looking out at my little port-hole, I saw the flying-fish, and the whales spouting, and the stormy-petrels and gulls.

On Sunday the boat was turned about; and

when we inquired why, we were told that the wind and sea were so much against us, we were going to put back into Crescent City. It came at once into our minds, how on Sunday, three years before, the steamer "Brother Jonathan," in attempting to do the same thing, struck a rock, and foundered, and nearly all on board were lost.

Crescent City is an isolated little settlement, a depot for supplies for miners working on the rivers in Northern California. It has properly no harbor, but only a roadstead, filled with the wildest-looking black rocks, of strange forms, standing far out from the shore, and affords a very imperfect shelter for vessels if they are so fortunate as to get safely in. The Coast Survey Report mentions it as "the most dangerous of the roadsteads usually resorted to, filled with sunken rocks and reefs." It further says, that "no vessel should think of gaining an anchorage there, without a pilot, or perfect knowledge of the hidden dangers. The rocks are of peculiar character, standing isolated like bayonets, with their points just below the surface, ready to pierce any unlucky craft that may encounter them." The "Dragon Rocks" lie in the near vicinity, at the end of a long reef that makes out from Crescent City. All the steamers that enter or depart from there must pass near them.

It is very remarkable, that, while the Atlantic coast abounds in excellent harbors, on the Pacific side of the continent there is no good harbor where a vessel can find refuge in any kind of weather between San Francisco Bay and San Diego to the south, and Port Angeles, on the Straits of Fuca, to the north. It is fitly characterized by Wilkes as an "iron-bound coast."

We reached here Saturday night. Sunday morning, hearing a silver triangle played in the streets, we looked out for tambourines and dancing-girls, but saw none, and were presently told it was the call to church. We were quite tempted to go and hear what the service would be, but the sound of the breakers on the bar enchained us to stop and listen to them.

PORTLAND, ORE., Oct. 20, 1868.

In coming up the river from Astoria, we had always in view the snow-white cone of St. Helen's, one of the principal peaks of the Cascade Range. Nothing can be conceived more virginal than this form of exquisite purity rising from the dark fir forests to the serene sky. Mount Baker's symmetry is much marred by the sunken crater at the summit; Mount Rainier's outline is more complicated: this is a pure, beautiful cone. It is so perfect a picture of heavenly calm, that it is as hard to realize its being volcanic as it would be to imagine an outburst of passion in a seraph. Frémont reports having seen columns of smoke ascending from it, and showers of ashes are known to have fallen over the Dalles.

As we approached Portland, the sharp-pointed form of Mount Hood came prominently into view. Portland would be only a commonplace city, the Willamette River being quite tame here, and the shores low and unattractive; but this grand old mountain, and the remnant of forest about it, give it an ancient, stately, and dignified look.

OLYMPIA, Oct. 30, 1868.

In crossing from the Columbia River to the Sound, we saw, along the Cowlitz Valley, marks of the havoc and devastation caused by the floods of last winter. The wild mountain stream had swept away many familiar landmarks since we were last there; in fact, had abandoned its bed, and taken a new channel. It gave us a realizing sense of the fact that great changes are still in process on our globe. Where we had quietly slumbered, is now the bed of the stream. We mourned over the little place at Monticello, where for eight years a nice garden, with rows of trim currant-bushes, had gladdened the eyes of travellers, and the neat inn, kept by a cheery old Methodist minister, had given them hospitable welcome, — not a vestige of the place now remaining. Civilization is so little advanced in that region, that few men would have the heart or the means to set out a garden.

# IX.

**Victoria. — Its Mountain Views, Rocks, and Flowers. — Vancouver's Admiration of the Island. — San Juan Islands. — Sir James Douglas. — Indian Wives. — Northern Indians. — Indian Workmanship. — The Thunder-bird. — Indian Offerings to the Spirit of a Child. — Pioneers. — Crows and Sea-birds.**

VICTORIA, B.C., Nov. 15, 1868.

WE are to stay for several months in this place. We are delightfully situated. The house has quite a Christmas look, from the holly and other bright berries that cluster round the windows. The hall is picturesquely ornamented with deer's horns and weapons and Indian curiosities. But the view is what we care most about. On our horizon we have the exquisite peaks of silver, the summits of the Olympic Range, at the foot of which we lived in Port Angeles. We look across the blue straits to them. Immediately in front is an oak grove, and on the other side a great extent of dark, Indian-looking woods. There are nearer mountains, where we can see all the beautiful changes of light and shade. Yesterday they were wrapped in haze, as in the Indian summer, and every thing was soft and dreamy about them; to-day they stand out bold and clear, with great wastes of snow, ravines, and land-slides, and dark prominences, all distinctly defined. When the setting sun lights up the summits, new fields of crystal and gold, and other more distant mountains, appear.

It is very refreshing to get here, the island has such a rich green look after California. It is quite rocky about us; but the rocks even are carpeted deep with moss, and the old gnarled branches of the oaks have a coating of thick, bright velvet. It is now the middle of November; and the young grass is springing up after the rain, and even where it does not grow there is no bare earth, but brown oak-leaves and brakes, with soft warm colors, particularly when the sun strikes across them. The skies, too, are like those at home, with the magnificent sunrise and sunset that only clouds can give. The California sky is, much of the time, pure unchanging blue.

When we first landed here, we were very much impressed by the appearance of the coast, it being bold and rocky, like that of New England; while on the opposite side of the straits, and almost everywhere on the Sound, are smooth, sandy shores, or high bluffs covered with trees. The trees, too, at once attracted our attention,—large, handsome oaks, instead of the rough firs, and a totally different undergrowth, with many flowers wholly unknown on the opposite side, which charmed us with their brilliancy and variety of color; among them the delicate cyclamen, and others that we had known only in greenhouses. They continually recalled to us the surprise of some of the early explorers at seeing an uncultivated country look so much like a garden. We were told that much less rain falls here than on the American side; the winds depositing their moisture as snow on the mountains before they reach Victoria, which gives it a dryer winter climate.

Vancouver, in his narrative, repeatedly speaks of the serenity of the weather here, and says that the scenery recalled to him delightful places in England. He felt as if the smooth, lawn-like slopes of the island must have been cleared by man. Every thing unsightly seemed to have been removed, and only what was most graceful and picturesque allowed to remain. He says, "I could not possibly believe that any uncultivated country had ever been discovered exhibiting so rich a picture." When requested by the

Spanish Seignor Quadra to select some harbor or island to which to give their joint names, in memory of their friendship, and the successful accomplishment of their business (they having been commissioned respectively by their governments to tender and receive the possessions of Nootka, given back by Spain to Great Britain), he selected this island as the fairest and most attractive that he had seen, and called it the "Island of Quadra and Vancouver." The "Quadra," as was usual with the Spanish names, was soon after dropped.

Between Vancouver's Island and Washington Territory lie the long-disputed islands of the San Juan group; the British claiming that Rosario Strait is the channel indicated in the Treaty of 1846, which would give them the islands; while the United States claim that De Haro Strait is the true channel, and that the islands belong to them.

These islands are valuable for their pasturage and their harbors, and most of all for their situation in a military point of view. While this question is still in dispute, the British fort at one end of San Juan, and the American fort at the other, observe towards each other a respectful silence.

DEC. 1, 1868.

Sir James Douglas, the first governor of British Columbia, selected the site of Victoria. Owing to his good taste, the natural beauty of the place has been largely preserved. The oak groves and delicate undergrowth are a great contrast to the rude mill-sites of the Sound, where every thing is sacrificed to sending off so much lumber. He lives at Victoria in a simple, unpretending way. It was made a law in British Columbia, that no white man should live with an Indian woman as wife, without marrying her. He set the example himself, by marrying one of the half-breed Indian women. Some of the chief officers of the Hudson Bay Company did the same. The aristocracy of Victoria has a large admixture of Indian blood. The company encouraged their employés, mostly French Canadians, to take Indian wives also. They were absolute in prohibiting the sale of intoxicating drinks to the Indians, and dismissed from their employ any one who violated this rule. They gave the Indians better goods than they got from the United-States agents; so that they even now distinguish between a King George (English) blanket, and a Boston (American) blanket, as between a good one and a bad one.

It was, no doubt, owing to the influence of Sir James Douglas, that Lady Burdett Coutts sent out and established a high school here for boys and girls.

Dec. 5, 1868.

We saw here some of the Northern Indians of the Haidah tribe, from Queen Charlotte's Islands. They came in large canoes, some of which would hold a hundred men, and yet each was hollowed out of a single log of cedar. They came down to bring a cargo of dogfish-oil to the light-house at Cape Flattery. They camped for two weeks on the beach, and we went often to see them. Having led such an isolated life on their islands, surrounded by rough water, and hardly known to white men, they have preserved many peculiarities of their tribe, and are quite different in their looks and habits from the Indians of Puget Sound. Some of the old women had a little piece of bone or pearl shell stuck through the lower lip, which gave them a very barbarous appearance; but in many ways the men had more knowledge of arts and manufactures than any other Indians we have seen. They showed us some ornaments of chased silver, which they offered for sale; also bottle-shaped baskets, made of roots and bark, so closely woven together as to hold water. But most curious to us were some little black, polished columns, about a foot high, that looked like ebony. They were covered with carvings, very skilfully executed. When we took them into our hands, we were surprised at their weight, and found that they were made of a fine, black coal-slate. A man who stood by explained to us that this slate is a peculiar product of their islands. When first quarried, it is so soft as to be easily cut; and when afterward rubbed with oil, and exposed to the air, it becomes intensely hard. At the foot of the column was the bear, who guards the entrance of their lodges; at the top, the crow, who presides over every thing. On some were frogs and lizards. One was surmounted by the "thunder-bird," a mythological combination of man and bird, who lives among the mountains. When he sails out from them, the sky is darkened; and the flapping of his wings makes the thunder, and the winking of his eyes the lightning. It is very strange that the "thunder-bird" should be one of the deities of the Indians of the North-west, where thunder is so rare as to be phenomenal. We heard of him in other parts of British Columbia, and see him represented in carvings from Sitka. Tatoosh Island, off Cape Flattery, where the Makah Indians live, derives its name from *Tootootche*, the Nootka name for the "thunder-bird." The Makahs originally came from the west coast of Vancouver's Island. They deem themselves much superior to the tribes of the interior, because they go out on the ocean. Their home being on the rocky coast islands, they naturally look to the water to secure their living. Their chief business is to hunt the whale, they being the only Indians who engage in this pursuit.

Sometimes we found the Indians so deeply interested in a game they were playing, that they took no notice of us. It was played with slender round sticks, about six inches long, made of yew wood, so exquisitely polished that it had a gloss like satin. Some of the sticks were inlaid with little bits of rainbow pearl, and I saw one on which the figure of a fish was very skilfully represented. It is quite incomprehensible, how they can do such delicate work with the poor tools they have. They use only something like a cobbler's knife.

They shuffled the sticks under tow of cedar-bark, droning all the time a low, monotonous chant. It is curious that any thing so extremely simple can be so fascinating. They will sit all day and night, without stopping for food, and gamble away every thing they possess. It appeared to be identical with the old game of "Odd or Even" played by the ancient Greeks, as described by Plato.

We saw here the great conical hat worn by the Cape-Flattery Indians, similar in form to the Chinese hat; and also some blankets of their own manufacture, woven of dog's hair.

PORT TOWNSEND, WASHINGTON TERRITORY,
April 4, 1869.

This afternoon we rode past the grave-yard of the Indians on the beach. It is a picturesque spot, as most of their burial-places are. They like to select them where land and water meet. A very old woman, wrapped in a green blanket, was digging clams with her paddle in the sand. She was one of those stiff old Indians, whom we occasionally see, who do not speak the Chinook at all, and take no notice whatever of the whites. I never feel as if they even see me when I am with them. They seem always in a deep dream. Her youth must have been long before any white people came to the country. When she dies, her body will be wrapped in the tattered green blanket, and laid here, with her paddle, her only possession, stuck up beside her in the sand.

We saw two Indians busy at one of the little

huts that cover the graves. They were nailing a new red covering over it. We asked them if a chief was dead. A *klootchman* we had not noticed before looked up, and said mournfully, "No," it was her "little woman." I saw that she had before her, on the sand, a number of little bright toys, — a doll wrapped in calico, a musical ball, a looking-glass, a package of candy and one of cakes, a bright tin pail full of sirup, and two large sacks, one of bread, and the other of apples.

Another and older woman was picking up driftwood, and arranging it for a fire. When the men had finished their work at the hut, they came and helped her. They laid it very carefully, with a great many openings, and level on the top, and lighted it.

Then the grandmother brought a little purple woollen shawl, and gave it to the old man. He held it out as far as his arm could reach, and waved it, and apparently called to the spirit of the child to come and receive it; and he then cast it into the fire. He spoke in the old Indian language, which they do not use in talking with us. It sounded very strange and thrilling. Each little toy they handled with great care before putting it into the flames. After they had burned up the bread and the apples, they poured on some sugar, and smothered the flames, making a dense column of smoke.

Then they all moved a little farther back, and motioned us to also. We wondered they had tolerated us so long, as they dislike being observed; but they seemed to feel that we sympathized with them. The old man staid nearest. He lay down on the sand, half hidden by a wrecked tree. He stripped his arms and legs bare, and pulled his hair all up to the top of his head, and knotted it in a curious way, so that it nodded in a shaggy tuft over his forehead. Then he lay motionless, looking at the fire, once in a while turning and saying something to the women, apparently about the child, as I several times distinguished the word *tenas-tenas* (the little one). I thought perhaps he might be describing her coming and taking the things. At times he became very animated. They did not stir, only answered with a kind of mournful "Ah — ah," to every thing he said.

At last their little dog bounded forward, as if to meet some one. At that, they were very much excited and pleased, and motioned us to go farther off still, as if it were too sacrilegious for us to stay there. They all turned away but the old man, and he began to move in a stealthy way towards the fire. All the clumsiness and weight of a man seemed to be gone. He was as light and wiry as a snake, and glided round the old drift that strewed the sand, with his body prostrate, but his head held erect, and his bright eyes fixed on the fire, like some wild desert creature, which he appeared to counterfeit. The Indians think, that, by assuming the shape of any creature, they can acquire something of its power. When he had nearly reached the fire, he sprang up, and caught something from it. I could not tell whether it was real or imaginary. He held it up to his breast, and appeared to caress it, and try to twine it about his neck. I thought at first it was a coal of fire; perhaps it was smoke. Three times he leaped nearly into the flames in this way, and darted at something which he apparently tried to seize. Then he seemed to assure the others that he had accomplished his purpose; and they all went immediately off, without looking back.

April 20, 1869.

We are surprised to find so many New-England people about us. Many of those who are interested in the saw-mills are lumbermen from Maine. The two men who first established themselves in the great wilderness, with unbroken forest, and only Indians about them, are still living near us. They are men of resources, as well as endurance. A man who comes to do battle against these great trees must necessarily be of quite a different character from one who expects, as the California pioneer did, to pick up his fortune in the dust at his feet. I am often reminded of Thoreau's experience in the Maine woods. He says, "The deeper you penetrate into the woods, the more intelligent, and, in one sense, less countrified, do you find the inhabitants; for always the pioneer has been a traveller, and to some extent a man of the world; and, as the distances with which he is familiar are greater, so is his information more general and far-reaching."

May 30, 1869.

The gulls and crows give parties to each other on the sand, at low-tide. Farther out are the ducks, wheeling about, and calling to each other, with sharp, lively voices. It is curious to watch them, and try to understand their impulses. Sometimes they are all perfectly motionless, sitting in companies of hundreds, in the deepest calm; sometimes all in a flutter, tripping over the water, with their wings just striking it, uttering their shrill cry. They dive, but never come to shore. What one does, all the rest immediately do. Sometimes the whole little fleet is gone in an instant, and the water unruffled above them.

The prettiest among them is the spirit-duck, —its motion is so beautiful, as it breasts the little billows, or glides through the still water. Their bosoms are so like the white-caps, I have to look for their little black heads, to see where they are. Once in a while, a loon comes sailing along, in its slow, stately way, turning its slender, graceful neck from side to side, as if enjoying the scenery. We never see more than two of them together, and they generally separate soon.

# X.

Puget Sound and Adjacent Waters. — Its Early Explorers. — Towns, Harbors, and Channels. — Vancouver's Nomenclature. — Juan de Fuca. — Mount Baker. — Chinese "Wing." — Ancient Indian Women. — Pink Flowering Currant and Humming-Birds. — "Ah Sing."

PORT TOWNSEND, Sept. 10, 1869.

WE have been spending a day or two in travelling about the Sound by steamer, touching at the various mill-towns and other ports, where the boat calls, to receive and deliver the mails, or for other business. Every time we pass over these waters, we admire anew their extent and beauty, and their attractive surroundings, their lovely bays and far-reaching inlets, their bold promontorics and lofty shores, their setting in the evergreen forest, and the great mountains in the distance, standing guard on either side.

The early explorers who visited this part of the country evidently had a high appreciation of it, as their accounts of it show. Vancouver, who came in 1792, expressed so much admiration of these waters and their surroundings, that his statements were received with hesitation, and it was supposed that his enthusiasm as an explorer had led him to exaggeration. But Wilkes, who followed him many years afterwards, confirmed all that he had said, and, in his narrative, writes as follows regarding this great inland sea: —

"Nothing can exceed the beauty of these waters, and their safety. Not a shoal exists within the Straits of San Juan de Fuca, Admiralty Inlet, Puget Sound, or Hood's Canal, that can in any way interrupt their navigation by a seventy-four-gun ship. I venture nothing in saying there is no country in the world that possesses waters equal to these."

In another account Wilkes writes: "One of the most noble estuaries in the world; without a danger of any kind to impede navigation; with a surrounding country capable of affording all kinds of supplies, harbors without obstruction at any season of the year, and a climate unsurpassed in salubrity."

More recently the United-States Coast Survey Report of 1858 declares, that, "For depth of water, boldness of approaches, freedom from hidden dangers, and the immeasurable sea of gigantic timber coming down to the very shores, these waters are unsurpassed, unapproachable."

We were at first puzzled by the various names given to the different waters over which we travelled; but soon discovered, that, while the term "Puget Sound" is popularly applied to the whole of them, it properly belongs only to the comparatively small body of water lying beyond the "Narrows," at the southern end. and the arms and inlets that branch therefrom.

The great natural divisions of this system are: the Straits of Juan de Fuca, extending from the ocean eastward about eighty miles, and then branching into the vast Gulf of Georgia to the north, and Admiralty Inlet to the south; Hood's Canal, branching from the latter, on the west side, near the entrance, and running south-west about sixty miles; Possession Sound, branching from the east side, and extending north between Whidby Island and the mainland, as far as Rosario Straits; and Puget Sound, connected with the southerly end of Admiralty Inlet by the "Narrows."

We commenced our recent trip at Victoria, and crossed the Straits of Fuca, — through which the west wind draws as through a tunnel, — to Port Angeles. This place was named by Don Francisco Elisa, who was sent out to this region in 1791 by the Mexican Viceroy. Of course Don Francisco must compliment the Viceroy by giving his name to some important points. This royal personage had a string of ten proper names, besides his titles. These Don Francisco distributed according to his judgment. Being apparently a religious man, he was mindful also of the claims of saints and angels; and, when he reached the first good harbor on the upper coast, he called it *Puerto de los Angeles* (Port of the Angels).

Proceeding eastward, the next point of interest is New Dungeness, so called by Vancouver from its resemblance in situation to Dungeness on the British Channel. The harbor of this place, like that of Port Angeles, is formed by a long sand-spit that curves out from the shore. On account of this resemblance, Vancouver gave to Port Angeles the name of False Dungeness, thinking it might be mistaken for the other. But this name has been dropped, and the more poetical designation of the Spaniard retained. The pious Elisa called the long-pointed sand-spit at Dungeness "the Point of the Holy Cross."

The great body of water north of Vancouver's Island, which had not yet received its name, he called *Canal de Nuestra Señora del Rosario* (the Channel of Our Lady of the Rosary). When Vancouver, in the following year, gave his own name to the island, he called this body of water the Gulf of Georgia, in honor of George III., the reigning king of England. The name given by Elisa is still retained by the strait east of the De Haro Archipelago.

The next place at which we stopped was Port Townsend. This was named, by Vancouver, Marrowstone Point, from the cliff of marrowstone at the head of the peninsula; but this name was afterwards given to the headland on the opposite side of the entrance to Port Townsend Bay, to the south-east of the town, and the name of Townshend, one of the lords of the Admiralty, was given to the bay. The town afterwards took the same name, dropping the *h* from it. Admiralty Inlet commences here, and was named by Vancouver in honor of the Board of Admiralty for whom he sailed. Hood's Canal was named for another of the lord-members of the Board.

Opposite, across the inlet, to the north and east, lies Whidby Island, which Vancouver named for one of his lieutenants. It is a pity it could not have had some more poetic name, it is so beautiful a place; it is familiarly known here as the "Garden of the Territory." It was formerly owned and occupied by the Skagit Indians, a large tribe, who had several villages there, and fine pasture-grounds; their name being still retained by the prominent headland at the southern extremity of the island. I heard one of the passengers remark that there were formerly white deer there. I strained my eyes as long as it was in sight, hoping to see one of these lovely creatures emerge from the dark woods; but in vain. Wilkes says that the Skagit Indians had large, well-built lodges of timber and planks. But, since so many tribes have been swept away by the small-pox, most of them have lost their interest in making substantial houses, feeling that they have so little while to live. North of Whidby is Fidalgo Island, named for a Spanish officer. Between them is a narrow passage, called Deception Pass, very intricate and full of rocks, above and below the water, and most difficult to navigate, — in striking contrast to the waters of the Sound in general.

We called at Port Ludlow and Port Gamble, the latter on Hood's Canal, near the entrance, — *Teekalet* being its Indian name. Returning to Admiralty Inlet, we presently passed Skagit Head, at the entrance of Possession Sound, so named by Vancouver to commemorate the formal taking possession, by him, of all the territory around the Straits of Fuca and Admiralty Inlet, on the king's birthday.

We steamed serenely on, over the clear, still water, to Port Madison, and then crossed the inlet to Seattle. Thence we proceeded south, and passed Vashon Island, which has many attractive features. Quartermaster's Harbor, at the southern end, is a lovely place; and beautiful shells and fossils are to be found there. Occasionally we came across a great boom of logs, travelling down to some saw-mill; or a crested cormorant, seated on a fragment of drift, sailed for a while in our company. We passed on through the "Narrows," and entered Puget Sound proper, named for Peter Puget, one of Vancouver's lieutenants, who explored it.

All Vancouver's friends, patrons, and officers — lieutenants, pursers, pilots, and pilot's mates — are abundantly honored in the names scattered about this region. He appears, too, to have had a good appreciation of nature, and praised, in his report, the landscape and the flowers. He regarded somewhat, in his nomenclature, the natural features of the country; as in Point Partridge, the eastern headland of Whidby Island; Hazel Point, on Hood's Canal;

Cypress Island, one of the San Juan group; and Birch Bay, south of the delta of Fraser River.

The Spanish explorers in this region do not seem to have taken much pains to record and publish the result of their discoveries. Vancouver held on to his with true English grip, and often supplanted their names by others of his own choosing.

At night we reached Steilacoom, where there was formerly a military post. It has an imposing situation, with a fine mountain view; and there are some excellent military roads leading from it in various directions.

We spent a pleasant day at Olympia, which lies at the southern extremity of the Sound, and resembles a New-England village, with its maples shading the streets, and flower-gardens. It has an excellent class of people, as have the towns upon the Sound in general; and the evidences of taste and culture, which are continually seen, are one of the pleasantest characteristics of this new and thinly settled part of the country.

There are no saw-mills on the Straits of Fuca, and the slight settlements along its shores have scarcely marred their primitive wildness and beauty. The original forest-line is hardly broken; the deer still come down to the water's edge; and the face of the country has apparently not changed since Vancouver, nearly a hundred years ago, stooped to gather the May roses at Dungeness; or Juan de Fuca, two centuries earlier, "sailed into that silent sea," and looked round at the mountains, — not less beautiful, though more imposing, than those that lay about his own home on the distant Mediterranean.

DEC. 10, 1869.

We have just seen an English gentleman who came over to this country for the purpose of ascending Mount Baker, first called by the Spaniards *Montaña del Carmêlo.* He was three years in trying to get a small company to attempt the expedition with him. Indians do not at all incline to ascending mountains; they seem to have some superstitious fear about it. I believe this mountain has never been explored to any extent. He describes the colors of the snow and ice as intensely beautiful. He has travelled among the Alps, but saw an entirely new phenomenon on the summit of Mount Baker, — the snow like little tongues of flame. In the deep rifts was a most exquisite blue. On the last day's upward journey, they were obliged to throw away all their blankets, — as they were not able to carry any weight, — and depend on chance for the night's shelter. How well Fate rewarded them for trusting her! They happened at night upon a warm cavern, where any extra coverings would have been quite superfluous. It was part of the crater, but they slept quietly notwithstanding.

JAN. 15, 1870.

We have now a little Chinese boy to live with us; that is, he represents himself as a boy, but he seems more as if he were a most ancient man. He might have stepped out of some Ninevite or Egyptian sculpture. He is like the little figures in the processions on the tombs, and his face is perfectly grave and unchanging all the time. I feel about him, as I do about some of the Indians, — as if he had not only his own age, but the age of his race, about him.

There never could be any thing more inappropriate than that he should be named "Wing," for no creature could be farther from any thing light or airy. One reason, I think, why he seems so different from any of his countrymen that we have seen, is because he has never lived in a city, but only in a small village, which he says has no name that we should understand.

He works in the slowest possible way, but

most faithfully and incessantly, and never shows the slightest desire for any recreation or rest. Even the anticipation of the great national Chinese feast, which is to be celebrated next month, and which occurs only once in a thousand years, has failed to arouse any enthusiasm in him, and he is apparently quite indifferent to it.

Our goat has taken a great dislike to him, — I think just because he is so different from herself. She is always making thrusts at him with her horns, and trying to butt him over. But he preserves, even toward her, his uniform sweet manner; calls her a "sheep," entirely ignoring her rude, fierce ways; leads her to pasture every day, under great difficulties; and attempts to milk her, at the risk of his life. The serenity of these people is really to be envied; they go on their way so perfectly undisturbed, whatever happens.

April 20, 1870.

The tides are very peculiar here. Every alternate fortnight they run very low, and then the beach is uncovered so far out that we can take long rides on it, as far as the head of the bay.

We are very much entertained with seeing

the old Indian crones digging clams. They appear to be equally amused with us, and chuckle with delight as we pass. It seems very strange to see human beings without the least approach to any thing civilized or artificial, with the single exception of the old blankets knotted about them with pieces of rope; but when I compare them with civilized women of the same age, who are generally helpless, I see that they have a great advantage over them. They are out everywhere, in all weathers, and do always the hardest of the work. We meet them often in the woods, so bowed down under the loads of bark on their backs, that it looks as if the bark itself had a stout pair of legs, and were walking. Our horse is always frightened, and can never get used to them.

We can ride now for hours on the beach, looking at the water on one side, and on the other at the densely wooded bluffs, now most beautifully lighted up by the pink flowering currant. It is like the rhodora at home, in respect to coming very early, — the flowers before the leaves. At first it is of a delicate faint pink; but as the season advances it becomes very deep and rich in color, and contrasts most beautifully with the drapery of light-gray moss, and the dark fir-trees.

This flower attracts the humming-bird, and furnishes its earliest food. This delicate, tropical-looking little creature is the first bird to arrive; coming often in March from its winter home in California, where it lives on another species of flowering currant that blooms through the winter.

In making some excavations here, there have been found the bones and teeth of the American elephant, and with them a bone made into a wedge, such as the Indians here use in splitting wood; which seems to imply great antiquity for their race.

AUG. 10, 1870.

We have a new China boy, Ah Sing, who is very impulsive and enthusiastic, quite a different character from the unemotional Wing. He is almost too zealous to learn. R. began to teach him his letters, to make him contented. I hear him now repeating them over and over to himself, with great emphasis, while he is washing the clothes. He is so big and strong, that they come out with great force. A few nights ago, after everybody had gone to bed, he came down past our room, and went into the kitchen. R. followed him to see what was the matter, and, as the boy looked a little wild, thought perhaps he was going into a fit. He had seized the primer, and was flourishing it about and gesticulating with it; and finally R., who has a wonderful faculty for comprehending the Chinese, divined that he had gone to bed without a lesson, and could not sleep until he had learned something.

# XI.

Rocky-mountain Region. — Railroad from Columbia River to Puget Sound. — Mountain Changes. — Mixture of Nationalities. — Journey to Coos Bay, Oregon. — Mountain Cañon. — A Branch of the Coquille. — Empire City. — Myrtle Grove. — Yaquina. — Genial Dwellers in the Woods. — Our Unknown Neighbor. — Whales. — Pet Seal and Eagle. — A Mourning Mother. — Visit from Yeomans.

PORT TOWNSEND, NOV. 18, 1872.

WE had quite a pleasant journey back from the East, and saw some things we must have passed in the night on our trip thither. About the Rocky-mountain region we saw what appeared to be immense ruins; but they were really natural formations, resembling old castles, with ramparts and battlements and towers. I could not help feeling as if they must belong to some gigantic extinct race. On the wide, solitary plains they were most imposing.

At the Laramie Plains, where we stopped a while, we were so blinded by the glittering crystals of quartz and specks of mica, we could well understand why the name of the Glittering Mountains was first given to the Rocky-mountain Range.

We saw at Cheyenne a most curious cactus. Outside, it was only a green, prickly ball; inside, was a deep nest, filled with a cluster of pink blossoms.

We looked into the beautiful Blue Cañon — blue with mist. Hundreds of feet below us was the gliding silver line of a stream.

At one of our stopping-places was a team of buffalo and oxen working together. To see this chief Manitou of the Indians so degraded, was like seeing a captive Jugurtha.

We found great changes had taken place within a year between Columbia River and Puget Sound. Where we used to cross alone, in the deepest solitude of the forest, there were cars running, gangs of Chinamen everywhere at work, great burnt tracts, and piles of fire-wood. Once in a while a stray deer bounded by, and turned back to look at us, with pretty, innocent curiosity. And there were still some of the old trees left standing, gnarled and twisted, and so thickly coated with moss, that great ferns grew out of it, and hung down from the branches. What a pity to destroy the work of centuries, the like of which we shall never see again!

We saw to-day some of the pretty spotted sea-doves, that have just arrived to spend the winter with us. Puget Sound, with its mild climate, is their Florida or Bermuda. In early spring they return to the rocky lagoons of the North, to pair and breed.

DEC. 15, 1872.

With our wider range from the hill-top to which we have removed, we notice more how the appearance of the mountains changes with the changes of the sky. This morning they were all rose-color; and are now so ghostly, the snow like shrouds about them. Before, we had only single chains and solitary peaks; here, we look into the bosom of a mountainous country, and every change in the light reveals something new. Where we have many times looked without seeing any thing, at length some beautiful new outline appears in faint silver on the distant horizon. Heaven ought to be more real to us for living in sight of what is so inaccessible, and so full of beauty and mystery.

MARCH 9, 1873.

We are very much struck with the mixture of nationalities upon this coast. We were so fortunate as to secure last winter the services of a splendid great Swedish girl, the heartiest and healthiest creature I ever saw. There did not seem to be a shadow of any kind about her, nor any thing more amiss with her in any way than there is with the sunshine or the blue sky. All kinds of work she took alike, with equal readiness, and never admitted to her mind a doubt or anxiety on any subject.

We felt sorry enough, when we had had her only three weeks, to have the foreman of the mill come and beg us to release her. It seems they were engaged to be married when they left Sweden; but, being of thrifty natures, they had agreed to work each a year before settling down in marriage. The constant sight of her charms proved too much for him, and they decided that all they needed to begin life together was their wealth of affection and their exuberant health and spirits.

Her size may be imagined, when I mention that her lover brought up six rings in succession, to try to find one big enough to go over her finger. Finally he squeezed on the largest one he could obtain, as an absolutely essential ceremony to bind them together, and smiled with delight to see that it could never be taken off.

The only help we could find in her place, at

such short notice, was a Russian boy, lately arrived from Kodiac. When we first saw him, we were quite disheartened at his appearance, his mouth and eyes were so like those of a fish, and he seemed so terribly uncivilized. I attempted to intimate that I thought we could not undertake to do any thing with him. He seemed to suspect what I thought, — although he could not understand my words, — and took up a piece of paper, and wrote some Russian words on it. I asked him what they meant; and he said, "Jesus Christ, he dead; he get up again; men and devils he take them all up." I supposed the most civilized person he had ever seen was the priest; and, as the priest had taught him that, he thought it was a kind of introduction for him, and that I should feel it to be a bond of union between us. I did not feel quite so much as if he were a fish or a seal afterward. All the time, even over the hot cooking-stove, he kept his rough fur cap on his head. His great staring eyes rolled round in every direction; and he looked so utterly uncouth and so bewildered, that I doubted very much if he could ever be adapted to our needs.

To my great surprise, however, he learned very fast, stimulated by his curiosity to know about every thing. What made him appear so very stupid at first was, that he felt so strongly the newness of all his surroundings. After he learned to talk with us, he interested us very much with accounts of his own country, and with the letters he read us from his father, an old man of ninety, who had spent his life in charge of convicts in Siberia. He wrote his father that he was homesick; and the old man replied: "You homesick — work! work by and by make you strong!" His letters were directed only: "Son mine — George Olaf." He seemed to trust to some one on the way, to take an interest in their reaching him.

The boy generally set up his hymn-book in some place where he could occasionally glance at it, and chant his Russian hymns, while he was about his work. On the other side, the nurse sang Dutch songs to the baby.

JULY 1, 1873.

We have just returned from a long, rough journey in southern and western Oregon. We crossed the Coast Range of mountains, — not so high and snow-capped as the Cascades, but beautiful to watch in their variations of light and shade, always the shadows of clouds travelling over them, and mists stealing up through the dark ravines. A Dutchwoman — our fellow-passenger — was in ecstasies, exclaiming continually: "How beautiful is the land here! How *bracht* [bright]!" — noticing all the sunlighted places; but I was more attracted by the shadows. I heard another hard-looking woman say to a man, that she cried when she saw the hills, they were so beautiful. There was a deep welcome in them; something human and responsive seemed to fill the stillness. In these solitary places, remote from all other associations, it seems as if Nature could communicate more directly with us.

I noticed, more than I ever did before, the difference in the appearance and bearing of the flowers; how some seemed only to flaunt themselves, and others had so much more character. As we passed a little opening in the woods, a great dark purple flower, that was a stranger to me, fixed its gaze upon me so that I felt the look, as we sometimes do from human eyes. Any thing supernatural is so in keeping with these solitary places, I felt as if some one had assumed that form to greet me. There were some beautiful new flowers; among them a snow-white iris, which was very lovely. It seemed like a miracle that this fair little creature should come up so unsoiled out of the rough, black earth.

We crossed the mountain range through a cañon. The road wound round and round the sides of it, sometimes so narrow that it seemed hardly more than an Indian trail. We had a true California driver, who shouted out to us every few minutes, to hold on tight, or all to get together on one side, or something equally suspicious; but dashed on without any regard to danger. We were in constant expectation of being hurled to the bottom; but it quickened our senses to enjoy the beauty about us, to feel that any moment might be our last. We saw below us great trees that filled the cañon. They were so very tall, that it appeared as if, after having grown into what would be recognized everywhere as lofty trees, they had altered their views altogether as to what a tall tree really should be, and started anew. We did not wholly enjoy looking down at their great mossy arms, stretched out as if to receive us. Everywhere was the most exquisite fragrance, from the Linnæa and other flowers. At the bottom was a little thread of a brook. After we passed through the cañon, the brook came out, and went down the mountain side with us. It was very lively company. Sometimes it hid from us, but we could tell where it was, by the rushing of the water. Then it would appear again, whirling and eddying about the rocks. In some places, its bed was of pure, hard stone, with basins full of foam. Sometimes the rocks were covered with dark, rich moss. There were retired little falls in it, that seemed like nuns, so unregarding as they were of all the commotion about them. Then the whole body of water would gather itself up, and shoot down some rock, and cut like a sword-blade into the still water below. We shall long remember that little, leaping, dancing branch of the Coquille, that runs from the Coast Mountains to the sea.

Upon learning that we were approaching "Empire City," we attempted a hasty toilet,— as appropriate for entering a metropolis as circumstances would permit,—but we were kindly informed that we might spare ourselves the trouble, as the place consisted at present of but a single house; a carpenter having established himself there, and, with a far-seeing eye, given the place its name, and started a settlement by building his own dwelling, and a play-house in the woods for his little daughter.

We spent one night in a myrtle-grove. The trees leaned gracefully together, and the whole grove for miles was made of beautiful arched aisles. Coming from our shaggy firs, and the rough undergrowth that is always beneath them, to these smooth, glossy leaves, and clear, open spaces of fine grass, was like entering fairy-land, or the "good green wood" of the ballads. I looked for princes and lovers wandering among them, and felt quite transformed myself. The driver I regarded as a different man from that moment; to think that he should show so much good taste as to draw up for the night in that lovely place.

In coming from the mountain, we had to ride a good deal of the way without seeing where we were going; and once we found ourselves with a great roof over our heads, hollowed out of the solid rock, and covered with dripping maiden's-hair. All the rock about was like flint, and worn into strange shapes by the water.

One day we were accompanied quite a distance through the woods by a female chief, Yaquina. I think that she is a celebrated woman in Oregon, and that Yaquina Bay was named for her. She was mounted on a little pony, and riding along in a free and joyous way, looking about at the green leaves and the sunshine. I thought of Victoria with her heavy crown, that gives her the sick headache, and wondered how she would like to exchange with her.

We were quite interested in some of the people we saw, one of them especially,—a man whose house had no windows. We felt at first as if we could not stop with him; but he came out to our wagon, looking so bright and clean, and had such an air of welcome as he said, "We are not very well provided, but we are very accommodating," that we at once decided to stop, particularly as the driver said the horses could not possibly go enough farther to get to any better place that night. He ushered us in very hospitably, and looking round the room — the chairs being rather scarce — said, "There are plenty of seats—on the floor." I saw some books on a shelf, and, going to look at them, found "Mill's Logic," and "Tyndall on Sound," and several others, scientific and historical. We found him, as he said we should, eager to make us comfortable. He noticed that the baby did not look well, and went out into the woods, and cut down a little tree that he said would do her good, and urged us to take it with us. He said that he was generally called in by his neighbors, in case of sickness or accident. He had learned to help himself in most ways, as he came there originally with only fifty cents in his pocket.

Another old man, at the next stopping-place,

made a beautiful picture, as he sat inside his open door, in a great, rough, home-made arm-chair, with a black bear-skin for a pillow,—a large, strong man, with long, shining, silver hair. We were very much pleased to find that we were to spend the night there, he looked so interesting. All his talk was about fights with wild beasts and Indians, and cutting down the big trees, and making the terrible roads we had been over. There was a good deal of refinement and gentleness, too, about him. He had in his arms a dear little child. He had adopted her, he said, because his were all grown up. She seemed like a soft little bird, so timid and clinging.

When we came to see our accommodations, we were delighted to find every thing so clean and agreeable. We expressed our pleasure to him, and he said, "Yes; a woman, I think, will go a mile or two farther for a clean sheet; and even a man does not altogether like to be tucked into bed with a stranger;" which suggests what the customs are there.

DEC. 20, 1873.

We were startled to learn, a few days since, that one of our neighbors had been found dead, —a man about whom there had always been a good deal of mystery in the village. He lived alone, and never spoke of any relations or friends. He was a man of very courteous manners, but on this point he would allow no questions. There was no one to notify of his death, and nobody appeared to claim his property.

The first time we ever saw him, he was riding in the woods, on a handsome horse, with a bright scarlet blanket. He looked so picturesque, and there was so much grace and dignity about him, that I felt as if he did not belong anywhere about here. It seemed as if he might have come riding out of some foreign land, or some distant age,—like a knight going to a tournament.

When we came to know him, we could not help wondering what could induce him to live here. He was thought to be Southern, and it was generally supposed that some difficulties arising at the time of the war had brought him here. He seemed disposed to make the best of our dull life, and always had something that interested him to show us,—a new flower, or curious shell, or some pretty Indian child.

The last time we saw him was Saturday night. It must have been only a few hours before his death, but he appeared in his usual fine health. The next we knew of him was Monday morning, when some men who lived near us said that nothing had been seen of him since his light disappeared Saturday night. As he did not open his house, as usual, on Sunday, they said to themselves, "He does not like to be disturbed," and waited till Monday, when they went to the window; and the dog inside, hearing the noise, came and tore down the curtain, and went back and sat down beside his master, where he lay on the bed, and licked his face; and they saw that he was dead. He was tenderly buried by the people of the village, without religious ceremonies; but they dropped little green branches into his grave in the way of the Free Masons. I was surprised at the delicacy of feeling shown in regard to his desire to remain unknown, rude curiosity concerning any thing peculiar being everywhere so common.

MAY 20, 1874.

This afternoon we went out a little farther than usual in our boat, and saw a herd of whales in the distance, — great free creatures, puffing and snorting, spouting and frolicking, together. The boatman said that a flap from one of their tails would send our boat clean out of the water, and turned hastily about, hallooing in the wildest way, to keep them off.

On our way back we passed some deserted buildings on a sandy point. We inquired about them, and were told that they were the commencement of a city, originally called "New York;" but, having disappointed its founders, the Indian name of *Alki* (By and By) was given to it in derision.

We saw in the woods near here some magnificent rhododendrons, ten or twelve feet tall, covered with clusters of rose-colored flowers.

One of the boatmen has a pet seal that we sometimes take out in the boat with us. We put him occasionally into the water, feeling that he must be longing to go; but he always stays near the boat, and comes back if we whistle to him, and seems quite companionable. Who would have believed that one of these cold sea creatures could ever have been enticed into such intimacy? Our only idea of them, before this experience, had been of a little dark head here and there in the distance, in the midst of great wastes of water, where, as Lowell says, they—

> "Solemnly lift their faces gray,
> Making it yet more lonely."

One of the captains we sailed with told us that he had at one time a gray eagle he had tamed when young, that often took coasting-voyages with him, leaving the vessel occasionally, and returning to it, even when it had sailed many miles; never, by mistake, alighting on another craft instead of his. Sometimes, when out on a voyage to San Francisco, it would leave the vessel, and return to his house on Port Discovery Bay.

Oct. 15, 1874.

As we were passing along near the shore today, in our boat, we saw an Indian woman sitting alone on the beach, moaning, and dipping her hands continually in the water. Her canoe was drawn up beside her. We stopped, and asked her if any one was dead. She pointed to a square box [1] in the canoe, and said, "*mika tenas*" (my child). She said, afterwards, that she was as tall as I, and "*hyas closhe*" (so good)!

As the poor Indian mother looked round at the waves and the sky to comfort her, I thought, what is there, after all, that civilization can offer, beyond what is given by Nature alone, to every one in deepest need?

Yeomans, our old Port Angeles friend, called on us to-day. Every year since we left there,

[1] The crouching position, the favorite one of the Indians in life, is preserved by them in the disposition of their dead.

he has included us in his annual visit to the Seattle tribes. Each time we see him I think must be the last, he looks so very old; but every autumn brings him back, apparently unchanged. He seems to alter as slowly as the old firs about him. I am surprised always at his light tread; he bears so little weight on his feet, but glides along as if he were still in the woods, and would not have a leaf rustle.

# XII.

Puget Sound to San Francisco. — A Model Vessel. — The Captain's Relation to his Men. — Rough Water. — Beauty of the Sea. — Golden-Gate Entrance. — San Francisco Streets. — Santa Barbara. — Its Invalids. — Our Spanish Neighbors. — The Mountains and the Bay. — Kelp. — Old Mission. — A Simoom. — The Channel Islands. — A New Type of Chinamen. — An Old Spanish House.

San Francisco, March 20, 1875.

WE reached here last night, after a rough voyage from Puget Sound. We had all our worst weather first. After three or four days came a bright, clear morning, and the captain called me on deck to see the sunrise. It was all so changed, so beautiful, so joyous, — all around the exquisite green light flashing through the waves as they broke; and as far off as we could see, in every direction, the water leaping and tossing itself into spray. A strong wind had taken the vessel in charge; and it flew swiftly over the water, with no changes needed, no altering of sails, no orders of any kind, and nobody seemed to be about. The captain fixed me a hammock in a sail; and I lay there hour after hour, with no company but the warm, bright sunshine straying over the deck. I felt as if it were an enchanted vessel, on which I was travelling alone.

Cleopatra's barge could not have been more carefully kept. When the men came out to their daily work, all their spare moments were spent in polishing and cleaning every little tarnished or dingy spot. At first it used to seem to me like a wanton risk of life, with the vessel rearing and plunging so that we did not dare to stir on deck, to see them climb the tall masts, and cling there, scraping and oiling them, to bring out the veining of the wood. Perhaps it was partly as a discipline in steadiness, that they were directed to do it, — to get used to working at such a height. What a contrast to the tawdriness of the steamers we had been accustomed to, to see every thing about us made beautiful by exquisite neatness, done chiefly, too, for their own eyes! I saw, then, why the sunshine was so pleasant on the deck; it was because there was nothing about the vessel out of keeping with the pure beauty of nature. I felt safer, too, to think how all things, small and great, conformed to the laws of Heaven.

One day I asked the captain if he had many of the same men with him as on the last voyage we took with him. 'I remembered his pointing out to me then the fair, honest face of a young Swedish sailor at the wheel. He said most of his men made many voyages with him. I spoke of another captain, who told us his men were almost all new every time. He said that was generally the master's fault; that a captain should not speak to his men just the same in fair weather and in foul. I looked with interest, afterward, to see his management of them, and found that, while every thing went on smoothly, he took pains to converse with them, and to become somewhat acquainted with each man. Then, in emergencies, his brief, clear directions were immediately comprehended, and promptly obeyed. I began to understand the secret of his short voyages (for his vessel had the reputation of being the fastest sailer between San Francisco and the Sound): it was partly from his management of the ship, and partly from his management of the men.

We started in a snow-storm, and at first every thing seemed to be against us. He had told us that March was not generally a very quiet month on the water. We took a tug-boat to tow us out to the entrance of the Straits;

but, as the weather grew continually worse, the steamer was obliged to leave us, with wind dead ahead, and against that we had to beat out. As soon as we had made Cape Flattery, the wind changed, and became what would have been a good wind for getting out, but was just the opposite of what we wanted for going down the coast. These reverses the captain received with unruffled serenity; although he dearly delights in his quick trips, and was ready to seize with alacrity the least breath in his favor. After all, he made one of his best voyages, by the help of the strong, steady wind that drove him on at the last. It was perhaps as much, however, from his vigilance in watching when there was so little to take advantage of, and seizing all the little bits of help it was possible to get, as it was from the great help of that powerful wind; for other vessels that started with us, and even days before us, have not come in yet, and they all had the great wind alike.

R—— ventured to inquire of the captain one day, when we were beating about the mouth of the Straits, as to the feasibility of going into Neeah Bay, while it was yet possible to do so; but the captain said he preferred to beat about, and then he was ready to take advantage of the first chance in his favor, which he might lose if he were in shelter.

One day it was more than I could enjoy. The wind roared so loud, and the sound of the waves was so heavy, that I retreated to my berth, and lay down; but I could not keep my mind off the thought of how deep the water was under us. After a while I went on deck and sat there again, and the vessel began to plunge so that it seemed as if it were trying to stand upon one end. I felt so frightened that I thought I would speak to the captain, and ask him if he ever knew a lumber-vessel to tip over; and if I dared I would suggest that he should carry a little less sail. I knew that he was once on a vessel that turned bottom upward in the Straits, and he was left on the overturned hull for three days, in a snow-storm, before help came to him. I spoke to him, and he did not give me much of an answer; but, a little while after, he came to me, and said, "Are you able to go to the forward part of the ship with me? I should like to have you, if you can." So he helped me along to the bow, where it seemed almost too frightful to go, and said, "Kneel down;" and knelt down by me, and said, "Look under the ship." It was one of the most beautiful sights I ever saw, — such a height of foam, and rainbows over it. The dark water beside it seemed to be full of little, sharp, shining needles. I suppose it was moving so quickly that made the elongated drops appear so. Then he took me to the other side, that was in shadow; and there the water was whirled into the most beautiful shapes, standing out distinct from each other, from the swiftness of the motion, that held them poised, like exquisite combinations of snowflakes, only more airy.

Presently he said, "Men don't often speak of these things to each other, but I feel the beauty of it. Nights when the vessel is moving so fast, I come and watch here for hours and hours, and dream over it." When I thought about it afterward, I wondered how he could know that the way to answer my fear was to show me what was so beautiful. I was not afraid any more, whatever the vessel did.

Those three days and nights of lonely watching, floating about in the Straits, must have been a great experience to him, and made him different from what he would otherwise have been; certainly different from most men.

Before sunrise, yesterday morning, we passed the "Seal Rocks;" as the light just began to reveal a little of the dark, dreamy hills on each side of the long, beautiful entrance to the harbor. A flood of light filled it as we entered, and it must have looked just as it did when it was first named the "Golden Gate." All along, for miles, the water throws itself up into the air, and falls in fountains on the rocky shore. I cannot conceive of a more beautiful harbor in the world; and, as we were two or three hours in coming from the sea up to the city, we had time enough to enjoy it.

The southern headland of the entrance is Point Lobos (*Punta de los Lobos*, Point of Wolves); the northern, Point Bonita (Beautiful Point).

MARCH 25, 1875.

We could never have stepped out of our wilderness into a stranger city than this. From the variety of foreign names and faces that I see in the streets, I should think I were travelling over the whole world. On one side of us lives a Danish family, on the other a French. I walk along and look up at the signs,—"Scandinavian Society;" "Yang Tzy Association of Shanghae;" "Nuevo Continente Restaurant Mejicano;" "Angelo Beffa, Helvetia Exchange," with the white cross and plumed hat of Switzerland. One street is all Chinese, with shiny-haired women, and little mandarins with long cues of braided red silk. The babies seem to be dressed in imitation of the idol in the temple; their tight caps have the same tinsel and trimmings, and the resemblance their little dry faces bear to it is very curious.

Next to "Tung Wo," "Sun Loy," and "Kum Lum," come "Witkowski," "Bukofski," "Rowminski," — who keep Russian caviar, etc. Some day, when we feel a little tired of our ordinary food, we think of trying the caviar, or perhaps a gelatinous bird's nest, for variety.

Besides the ordinary residents, we meet many sailors from the hundreds of vessels always in the harbor, — Greeks, Lascars, Malays, and Kanakas. Their picturesque costumes and Oriental faces add still more to the foreign look of the place.

In the midst of the greatest rush and confusion of one of the principal business streets, stands a man with an electrical machine, bawling in stentorian tones, "Nothing like it to steady the nerves, and strengthen the heart," — ready, for a small fee, to administer on the spot a current of greater or less intensity to whoever may desire it. The contrast is most ludicrous between the need that undoubtedly exists for some such quieting influence, and the utter inefficacy of it, if applied, under such circumstances.

We have just returned from Santa Barbara. How buoyant the air seems, and how brisk the people, after our languid, dreamy life there! I, who went there in robust health, spent six months in bed, for no other reason, that I could understand, than the influence of the climate. Perhaps, on homœopathic principles, as Santa Barbara makes sick people well, it makes well people sick. A physician that I have seen since coming here tells me that he went there himself for his own health, and was so much affected by the general atmosphere of sickness, that he was obliged to return. It is a depressing sight, certainly, to see so many feeble, consumptive-looking people about, as we did there. Where we lived I think it was also malarious, from the *estero* that winds like a snake about the lowlands near the bay. The favorite part of the city is near the foot-hills. It is probably more healthful there, but we cannot live without seeing at least one little silver line of the sea. So we took up our abode in the midst of the Spanish population, near the water.

We found it very difficult to get any one to help us in our work, although we had supposed that in the midst of poor people we should be favorably situated in that respect. We were told, however, that the true Castilian, no matter how poor, never works; that we might perhaps find some one among the Mexicans to assist us.

Our neighbors were quite interesting to watch, and we were pleased with the simplicity of their lives. They had no apparent means of support, unless it might be lassoing and taming some wild mustangs, which they were sometimes engaged in doing; but this seemed to be more of a recreation than a business with them. They were never harassed nor hurried about any thing. They lived mostly outside their little dark dwelling, only seeking it at noon for a *siesta.* In the morning they placed a mat under the trees, and put the babies down naked to play on it, shaking down the leaves for playthings. Sometimes they cut a great piece of meat into narrow strips, and hung it all over our fence to dry. This dried meat, and melons, constituted a large part of their food. The old mother was called *Gracia*, but she could never in her youth have been more graceful than now. She was as picturesque still as she could ever have been, and perfectly erect. She wore a little black cap, like a priest's cap, on the top of her head, and her long gray hair floated out from it over her shoulders; and, with her black mantle thrown as gracefully about her as any young person could have worn it, we used to see her starting out every morning to enjoy herself abroad. She appeared one morning at our window, before we were up, with her arms full of roses covered with dew, eager to give them to us while they were so fresh.

We noticed her sometimes out in the yard, preparing some of the family food, by the aid of a curious flat stone supported on three legs, and a stone pestle or roller, — a very primitive arrangement. Kneeling down upon the ground, she placed her corn, or Chili peppers — or whatever article she wished to grind — upon the stone; and, taking the hand-stone, she rolled it vigorously back and forth over the flat surface, crushing up the material, which fell off at the lower end into a dish below. We saw her making *tomales*, composed of bruised green corn, — crushed by the process just described, — mixed with chopped meat, and seasoned with Chili peppers or other pungent flavoring, and made up into slender rolls, each enveloped in green-corn leaves, tied at the ends, and baked in the ashes, — resulting in a very savory article of food.

Our only New-England acquaintances at Santa Barbara had evidently modified very much their ideas of living. We found them with bare floors, a great bunch of pampas grass, and a guitar hanging against the wall, in true Spanish fashion; the room being otherwise mostly empty.

We had on one side the dark Santa Ynez Mountains, and on the other the sea. The mountains are not very high but bold in their outlines; and the number of crags and ravines gives them a beautiful play of light and shadow. Very early one morning I saw a great gray eagle fly overhead, back to his home in their dark recesses. Some of the slopes are covered with grape-vines, and some with olive-trees. Far up in the hollows can be seen the little white houses of the people who keep the bee-ranches. They live up so high because the flowers last longer there. The mountains form a semicircle on one side of the town; on the other is the beach. An immense bed of kelp, extending for miles and miles along the shore, forms the most beautiful figures, rising and falling as it floats on the water,—so gigantic, and at the same time so graceful. It is of every beautiful shade of pale yellow and brown. In winter the gales sometimes drive it shoreward in such vast quantities that vessels are compelled to anchor outside of it.

There is an old mission there, built in the

Moorish style, where all visitors are hospitably received by the Franciscan friars in charge. This mission, like all those we have seen, has a choice situation, sheltered from wind, and with good soil about it. The old monks knew how to make themselves comfortable. Their cattle roamed over boundless pastures, herded by mounted *vaqueros;* their grain-fields ripened under cloudless skies; their olive-orchards, carefully watered and tended by their Indian subjects, yielded rich returns.

We made the acquaintance of a gentleman from Morocco, who says that the climate there is almost the same as that of Santa Barbara. I suppose the simoom we had there in the summer was a specimen of it. A fierce, hot wind blew from the Mojave desert. There was no possibility of comfort in the house, nor out of it. We could escape the storm of wind and dust by going in, but there was still the choking feeling of the air. The residents of the place could say nothing in defence of it, — only that did not occur often.

We are told that on the 17th of June, 1859, there was much more of a genuine simoom. So hot a blast of air swept over the town as to fill the people with terror. This burning wind raised dense clouds of fine dust. Birds dropped dead from the trees. The people shut themselves up in their thick adobe houses. The mercury rapidly rose to 133 degrees, and continued so for three hours. Trees were blighted, and gardens ruined.

Sailors approaching the coast in a fog can recognize the Santa Barbara Channel by the smell of bitumen which floats on the water. Some of the old navigators thought their vessels were on fire when they noticed it. It gives a luminous appearance to the water at night.

On one side of Santa Barbara is a great table-land, called the *Mesa*, where there is always a sea-breeze that blows across fields of grain and fragrant grass. That would be a beautiful place to live, but there is no water. The experiment of artesian wells is about being tried.

From the *Mesa* we looked off to the channel islands, — Santa Cruz, Santa Rosa, San Miguel, and Anacapa, — bold, rocky, and picturesque. Anacapa was formerly a great resort for the seal and otter; and the natives from Alaska came down to hunt them, and collected large quantities of their valuable skins. The island is of sandstone, all honeycombed with cavities of different sizes, sometimes making beautiful arches. There is no water on this island,

and only cactus and coarse grass grow there. Others of the group have wood and water, and settlements of fishermen. On some of them, interesting historical relics have been discovered, — supposed to be the remains of a temple to the sun, with idols and images. There are also beautiful fossils and corals and abalone shells.

It was hard to make up our minds to leave so lovely a place ; but as I looked back, the last morning, to fix the picture of it in my mind, I saw the little white clouds that come before the hot wind, rising above the mountains, and was glad that we were going. Two immense columns of smoke rose out of the cañons, and stood over the place, like genii. In the dry weather it seems that the mountains are almost always on fire, which modifies what is called the natural climate of Santa Barbara, so as to make it very uncomfortable. Its admirers must come from some worse place, — probably often from the interior; no one from Puget Sound ever praises it. We met several families from that region; and they were all anxious to get back to the clear mountain atmosphere of their northern climate, which is as equable as that of Santa Barbara, though far different in character.

We saw there some Chinese quite unlike any that we have met before. We have heard that most of those who come to the Pacific Coast are of an inferior kind, chiefly Tartars. There we saw some quite handsome ones, who had more of an Arab look, and had also elegant manners, — one, especially, who had a little office near us. On the birthday of the Emperor of China, his room was ornamented with a picture of Confucius, before which he burned scented wood; and hanging over it was an air-castle, with the motto, " God is Love."

We visited one day an interesting-looking old house, near our quarter of the town, to see if we could live in it. It was one of the finest there before the place became Americanized, and belonged to an old Spanish don. It stands in the centre of spacious and beautiful grounds, and the avenue leading to it is bordered with olive-trees, which were in bloom. There was a curious, delicate fragrance in the air, quite new to me, which I attributed to them. It was as different from all other odors, as their color is from that of all other trees. They have a little greenish blossom, something like a daphne, and the foliage is of beautiful shades of gray-green, from an almost black to light silvery color. They seem like old Spaniards themselves, they have such an ancient, reserved look. Two magnificent pepper-trees, with their light, graceful foliage trailing from the branches, stand near the door. The house is shut in with dark heavp porches on all sides, and covered with vines. The windows are in such deep recesses, owing to the great thickness of the walls of the house, that the rooms were but dimly lighted, although it was early in the afternoon. Some of the windows are of stained glass, and others of ground glass, to lessen the light still more. It is an adobe house; and the walls are so damp that I gave up all idea of living in it, as soon as I laid my hand on them. The Spaniards, I see, all build their houses on a plan that originated in a hot country, where the idea of comfort was all of coolness and shade. This house, and the one opposite where we lived, are covered with passion-flowers. Near the latter are two dark evergreen-trees, — the Santa Cruz spruce, — trimmed so as to be very stiff and straight, standing like dark wardens before the door. There is a hedge of pomegranate, with its flame-like flowers, which seem to be filled with light. The pepper-tree abounds in Santa Barbara, and the eucalyptus is being planted a good deal. It has a special power to absorb malaria from the air, and makes unhealthy places wholesome.

# XIII.

Our Aerie. — The Bay and the Hills. — The Little Gnome. — Earthquake. — Temporary Residents. — The Trade-Wind. — Seal-Rocks. — Farallon Islands. — Exhilarating Air. — Approach of Summer. — Centennial Procession. — Suicides. — Mission Dolores. — Father Pedro Font and his Expedition. — The Mission Indians. — Chinese Feast of the Dead. — Curious Weather.

SAN FRANCISCO, Oct. 30, 1875.

WE have found a magnificent situation. Our little house is perched on such a height, that every one wonders how we ever discovered it. The site of the city was originally a collection of immense sandhills, on the sides and tops of which the houses were built, many of them before the streets were laid out and graded. When the grades were finally determined, and the hills cut through, — as some of them were, — houses were often left perched far above, on the edge of a cliff, and almost as inaccessible as a feudal castle. I feel as if ours might be an eagle's nest, and enjoy the wildness and solitude of it. So does our

Scotch shepherd dog, who has been used to lonely places. Sometimes, just as the sun is rising, we see him sitting out on the sandhills, looking about with such a contented expression that it seems as if he smiled. He opens his mouth to drink in the wind, as if it were a delicious draught to him.

The hills are covered with sage-brush, full of little twittering birds. My bed is between two windows, and they fly across from one to the other, without minding me at all. Opposite is Alcatraz, a fortified island, but very peaceful-looking, the waves breaking softly all around it. It has still the Spanish name of the white pelicans with which it used to be covered. The commander of the fort died since we came here, and was carried across the water, with music, to Angel Island, to be buried.

Across the bay is a low line of hills, with softly rounded outlines. They are of pale russet color, from the red earth, and thin, dried grass, that covers them. Farther to the north is Mount Tamalpias, with sharper outlines.

Nov. 8, 1875.

The China boys generally refuse to come out here to live with us, saying it is "too far, too far." The unsettled appearance of this part of the city does not please them. To-day we succeeded in securing a small one. He is a curious-looking little creature, with a high pointed head, stiff, black hair, and small, sparkling eyes. He seems like a little gnome, and might have been living in the bowels of the earth, in mines and caverns, with black coal and bright jewels about him. Before he would agree to come, he said he must go and consult the idol in the temple. He burned little fragrant sticks before him; but how he divined what his pleasure might be, I could not tell.

We hesitated about taking him, considering his very stunted appearance; but he said, "Me heap smart," and that settled it. "Heap" must be a word the Chinese have picked up at the mines. It is in constant requisition in any attempt to converse with them.

Last night we had a heavy shock of earthquake. How different it is from merely reading that the crust of the earth is thin, and that there is fire under it, to feel it tremble under your feet! I was glad to have one thing more made real to me, that before meant nothing. It was a strange, deep trembling, as if every thing were sliding away from us.

Nov. [illegible]

It gives one a lonesome feeling to see how many people have lead unsettled lives, looking upon some other place as their home. Even the children, hearing so much talk about the East, seem to have an idea that they really belong somewhere else. One of our little neighbors said to me, "I have never been home;" [illegible] she, and all her grown-up brothers and sisters were born and brought up here. Many of the customs of the place are adapted to a temporary way of living. In most parts of the city it would be hard to find a street without signs of "Furnished rooms to let." Besides numerous restaurants, a flying kitchen travels about, with every thing cooking as it goes along, and [illegible] men, with white aprons, to serve the food; one ringing a bell, and looking out in every direction, to see what is wanted.

The numerous windmills, for raising water, give the city a lively look. The wind keeps them always in motion. The constant whirling of the wheels and the general breezy look of things, distinguish this place from all others that I have seen. Sir Francis Drake, commander, [illegible] [illegible] nearly three hundred years ago, refers with great delight to "a friendly wind" that took him "into a safe and good bay." There was for a long time, some doctor is to [illegible] of seven years be made. I think that measure of the word settles it. The assertion would have been [illegible] with [illegible] vague ever since. In summer [illegible] the same as [illegible] it will carry a vessel up against the strongest tide.

The city is built mainly of wood. The absence of foliage, and the neutral color of the houses, gives the streets a dull gray look, here and there redeemed by the scarlet geranium, which, if not a native, is most thoroughly naturalized,—it grows so sturdily, even in the poorest yards.

April [illegible]

We had a long ride out to the Seal-Rocks, past great wavy hills, with patches of gold brighter than the dandelions and buttercups are at home. This was the eschscholtzia, or California poppy. Occasionally we passed great tracts of lupine. The lowland was a sea of blue iris.

Suddenly, as we surmounted a height, the ocean rolled in before us, line after line of breakers, on a broad beach. When we reached Point Lobos we saw the two great rocks, far out in the water, covered with brown seals that lay in the sun like flocks of sheep, and [illegible] slippery, shining ones all the time crawling up out of the water, and dropping back again. As the vessels pass out of the bay, they go near enough to hear them bark; but nothing frightens them away, nor discomposes them in the least, although they are only a few miles from the city, and have a great many visitors. They are protected by law from molestation.

We looked off to the Farallon Islands, which are one of the chief landmarks for vessels approaching the Golden Gate. There was formerly a settlement of Russians there, who hunted the seal and the otter. These islands are still a great resort for seals, also for comorants and sea-gulls; and the large speckled eggs of the birds are gathered in quantities, and brought to the San Francisco market for sale. They were called by the Spaniards "*Farallons de los Frayles*" (Islands of the Friars), *farallon* being a sharp-pointed island.

There is a marvellous exhilaration in the air. The enthusiastic Bayard Taylor said, that, in in his first drive round the bay, he felt like Julius Cæsar, Milo of Crotana, and Gen. Jackson, rolled into one. It is an acknowledged fact, that both men and animals can work harder and longer here, without apparent injury or fatigue, than anywhere on the Eastern coast.

We have heard it suggested that the abundant actinic rays in the dry, cloudless atmosphere are the cause of this invigoration, and also of the unusual brilliancy of the flowers.

JUNE 1, 1876.

The only way in which we know that summer is coming is by the more chilling winds, the increased dust, the tawny color of the hills, and the general dying look of things. Every thing is bare, sunny, and sandy.

We are surrounded with great wastes of sand, which the wind drives against the house, so that it seems always like a storm. Sometimes, when I sit at work at the window, a gopher comes out of the sandhill, and sits down outside it. His company makes me feel still more remote from all civilized things.

JULY 4, 1876.

We had a splendid Centennial procession. Things that we imitate at home are all real here. Instead of having our own people dressed up in foreign costume, we have Italians, French, Swiss, Russians, Germans, Chinese, Turks, etc., all ready for any occasion. The newspapers mentioned as a remarkable fact, that there were no suicides for a week beforehand; every one seemed to have something to look forward to.

The night before the celebration, the French residents built up a great arch, as high as the highest buildings, with fine decorations, for the procession to pass under. Some doubt was expressed about the Germans liking to pass beneath the French arch; so three thousand Germans, to show their good-will, went and sung the Marseillaise under it.

The Jews have the handsomest church in San Francisco, which they decorated with the greatest enthusiasm, and had Centennial services, in which they said that they, of all people in the world, ought to appreciate America, as, before they came here, they were outcasts everywhere, while here they were unmolested and prosperous.

I liked best in the procession the Highlanders, who were real Scotchmen, in plaids, and bonnets with eagle feathers. Every one had a claymore by his side, and a thistle on his breast; and there were pipers playing on bagpipes to lead them.

There are a great many Germans in San Francisco, and the brewers had a car dressed with yellow barley and other ripe grains. The great fat men looked so full of enjoyment, it was really picturesque to see them, under the nodding grain. For the first time in my life I appreciated them, as I saw how poorly a thin man would convey the idea of comfort. There are a good many Italian fishermen here too. They are always just fit for processions, without any alteration whatever; their pretty green boat "Venezia," and their Captain Cæsar Celso Morena, seem made for it. They had Roman guards, in golden scale armor. The California Jaegers with their wild brown faces, that seemed to transport us to the great hot plains where they herd and lasso the half-tamed animals, walked too in the procession; and the baby camel, born lately in San Francisco, a great pet. They were led by the silver cornet band, whose music was exquisitely clear and sweet.

Aug. 2, 1876.

In this homeless city, built upon sandhills, and continually desolated by winds, it is no wonder that the blue bay looks attractive, especially to any one thrust aside in the continual vicissitudes of this unsettled life. The first news we heard, on our return from Santa Barbara, was that Ralston, the great banker, and one of the chief favorites in social life, had sought the calm of its still depths as better than any thing life could offer. How serenely the water lay in the sunshine, as we looked at it, hearing this news, which had stirred the city to its utmost! Here all secrets are guarded, all perplexities end. The passion for suicide seeks mostly this pathway, though there is an unprecedented number of intentional deaths of all kinds.

This morning's paper records the suicide of a Frenchman, who half reconciled me to his view, by the cheerful, intelligent way in which he spoke. He left a letter stating that he died with no ill feeling toward any one, and full of faith in God as a Father; that he did not consider that he was to blame for what he was about to do, as he had tried in vain to get work, — probably because he was wholly deaf. He made so little fuss about what almost every one would have considered a terrible calamity, — that his life should end in this way, — that it seemed a pity it could not otherwise have been made known what kind of a man he was. He gave a little account of himself, beginning, "I was born in the province of Haute Vienne, in France, and have lived mostly at the mines," going on to speak as quietly of what he was about to do, as he might if he were going to move from one town to another, not having succeeded in the first; ending by saying, "I have taken the poison, — an acid taste, but not disagreeable." He made only one request, — that a package of old letters should be laid on his breast, and buried with him. A valuable member of society might have been saved, if the result in his case could have been the same as with a man we knew in Santa Barbara, who, becoming discouraged by continual rheumatism, combined with poverty, took a large dose of strychnine, with suicidal intent, but, to his astonishment, was entirely cured of his rheumatism; and the notoriety he acquired presently procured him an abundance of work.

In the winter a man who called himself Professor Blake, a "mind-reader," gave some exhibitions of his power, which were considered wonderful. It might have been better for him, however, not to know what people thought, as it proved. A few weeks ago a man was discovered dead, with this letter beside him: "I die of a weary and a heavy heart, but of a sound mind. If there should be one or two persons to whom I should be known, let them, out of charity to the living, withhold their knowledge. Should my eyes be open, close them, that I may not chance, even in death, to see any more of this hated world." Notwithstanding his wish, of course every effort was made to find out who he was; and it proved to be this "mind-reader."

These cases are very depressing to think of; only that it makes one feel more certain of another life, to see how unfinished and unsatisfactory some things are here.

SEPT. 6, 1876.

I have found two beautiful places to visit, — the old Spanish graveyard of the Mission Dolores, and Lone Mountain Cemetery. They have long, deep grass, and bright, exquisite flowers. On the waste tracks about the cemetery, I can still find the fragrant little *yerba buena* (good herb), from which the Spanish Fathers named the spot where San Francisco now stands, in the primitive times, long before gold was discovered. The cross on the summit of Lone Mountain, erected by the Franciscan friars, is quite impressive from its height and size. It is seen from all parts of the city.

The Mission Dolores (Mission of our Lady of Sorrow) is south of the city, sheltered from the wind, with a clear stream flowing near. The fathers displayed their customary shrewdness in the selection of this situation. The bleak sandhills to the north they left for the future city, and settled themselves in this pleasant valley. The pioneer missionary of Northern California — Father Junipero Serra, that rigorous old Spaniard who used to beat his breast with stones — established himself here, with his Franciscan monks, in the fall of 1776. His old church is still standing, — an adobe building, with earthen floor, the walls and ceiling covered with rude paintings of saints and angels.

The Presidio of San Francisco was established in the spring preceding, by a colony sent out by the Viceroy of Mexico, accompanied by a military command. Father Pedro Font came with the expedition. He was a scientific man, and recorded his observations of the country and the people. Just before starting, a mass was sung for their happy journey, to the Most Blessed Virgin of Guadalupe, whom they chose for their patroness, together with the Archangel Michael and their Father Saint Francis.

When they reached the vicinity of the Gila River, the governors of several of the rancherias came out to meet them, with the alcalde, and a body of Pimas Indians, mounted on horses, who presented them with the scalps of several Apaches they had slain the day before. At the next stopping-place along the river, they were met by about a thousand Indians, who were very hospitable, and made a great shed of green boughs for them, in which to pass the night.

Father Pedro observed that the country must formerly have been inhabited by a different race, as the ground was strewn with fragments of painted earthenware, which the Pimas did not understand making. He saw also the ruins of an ancient building, with walls four and six feet thick. On the east and west sides were round openings, through which, according to the Indian traditions, the prince who lived there used to salute the rising and setting sun.

The company travelled on, singing masses, and resting by the way, until they reached what Father Pedro called "a miracle of Nature, the port of ports" (San Francisco Bay). He ascended a table-land, that ended in a steep white rock, to admire what he calls the "delicious view,"—including the bay and its islands, and the ocean, with the *Farallons* in the distance, of which he made a sketch. He mentioned Angel Island, which still bears that name. The commandant planted a cross on the steep white rock, as the symbol of possession, and also at Point Reyes (Point of Kings), and selected the table-land for the site of the Presidio. Father Font explored the country about the bay, and made some surveys. He noticed some Indians with launches made of *tules* (bulrushes), in which they navigated the streams.

It would have been fortunate for the Indians if all the priests sent among them had been of as gentle a spirit as Father Pedro. He says, in his account of this expedition, that they received him everywhere with demonstrations of joy, with dancing and singing. But, some years after, we hear that the soldiers were sent out from the Presidio to lasso the Indians. They were brought in like wild beasts, immediately baptized, and their Christianization commenced. Kotzebue, one of the early Russian explorers, says that in his time (1824) he saw them at Santa Clara driven into the church like a flock of sheep, by an old ragged Spaniard, armed with a stick. Some of the more humane priests complained bitterly of this violent method of converting the heathen, and insisted that all the Indians who had been brought in by force should be restored "to their gentile condition."

In the old Mission of Santa Barbara, we saw some of the frightful pictures considered so very effective in converting them. One special painting, representing in most vivid colors the torments of hell, was said of itself alone to have led to hosts of conversions; but a picture of paradise, in the same church, which was very subdued in its treatment and coloring, had failed to produce any effect.

The services of the Indians belonged for life to the missions to which they were attached. They were taught many useful things. They watered and kept the gardens and fields of grain, and tended the immense herds of cattle that roamed over the hills. Traders came to the coast to buy hides and tallow from the ranches and the missions, and the product of their fields. For seventy years, these old monks, supported by Spain, were the rulers of California. Spain's foreign and colonial troubles, however, led her to appropriate to other purposes the "Pious Fund" by which the missions were maintained. Jealousy of their growing power, and revolutions in Mexico, hastened their downfall. The discovery of gold in 1848 introduced the element which was to prove their final destruction.

It is a curious fact that the first adventurer who ever set foot on this soil, Sir Francis Drake, although he was here for only a month, repairing his ship, became convinced that there was no earth about here but had some probable show of gold or silver in it. If news had spread then as rapidly as now, in these days of newspapers and telegraphs, it would not have lain two hundred and seventy years untouched, and then been discovered only by accident.

Nov. 3, 1876.

A few days ago, I wandered on to the solitary Chinese quarter of Lone Mountain, and happened upon the celebration of the Feast of the Dead. Hundreds and hundreds of Chinamen were bowing over the graves in the sand. Each grave had on it little bright-colored tapers burning, sometimes large fires beside, made of the red and silver paper they use at the New Year. Each had curious little cups and teapots and chop-sticks, rice, sugar-cane, and roast chicken. I saw some little white cakes, inscribed with red letters, similar to children's Christmas cakes with names on them. Every thing that seems nice to a Chinaman was there. They were so engrossed in what they were doing, that they took no notice whatever of my observation of them. At each grave they spread a mat, and arranged the food. Then some one that I took for the nearest friend clasped his hands, and bowed in a sober, reverent way over the grave; then poured one of the little cups of rice wine out on the sand. It reminded me of the offerings I saw made to the spirit of the dead Indian child, at Port Townsend. Then two dead men were brought out to be buried, while we stood there; and the instant they were covered with the sand, the Chinamen called to each other, "fy, fy!" (quick, quick!), — to light the fire, as if it were to guide them on the way, as the Indians think. They threw into the air a great many little papers. I asked if those were letters to the dead Chinamen, and they said, "Yes," — but I am not sure if they understood me.

It produced such a strange effect, in this wild, desert-looking place, to see all these curious movements, and the fires and the feasts on the graves, that I felt utterly lost. It was as if I had stepped, for a few moments, into another world.

The Chinamen are so very saving, never wasting any thing, and they have to work so hard for all their money, and pay such high duty on the things they import from home, that they would not incur all this expense unless they felt sure that it answered some end. It is a matter for endless pondering what they really believe about it. They are satisfied with a very poor, little, frugal meal for themselves; but on this occasion every thing was done in the greatest style. At one place was a whole pig, roasted and varnished; and every grave had a fat, roasted chicken, with its head on, and dressed and ornamented in the most fanciful manner. The red paper which they use for visiting-cards at the New Year, and seem to be very choice of then, they sacrificed in the most lavish way at this time. They fired off a great many crackers to keep off bad spirits.

Most of the graves were only little sand-mounds for temporary use, until the occupants should be carried back to China; but one was a great semi-circular vault, so grand and substantial-looking that it suggested the Egyptian Catacombs. Over one division of the grave-yard, I saw a notice which I could partly read, saying that no woman or child could be buried there.

The Chinese are so out of favor here now, that the State Government is trying to limit the number that shall be allowed to come. About a thousand arrive on each steamer. How foolish it seems to be afraid of them, especially for their good qualities! the chief complaint against them being that they are so industrious, economical, and persevering, that sooner or later all the work here will fall into their hands.

JAN. 9, 1877.

We have been having some very strange weather here, — earthquake weather, it is called by some persons. It seems as if it came from internal fires. It has been so warm at night that we could not sleep, even with two open windows.

The chief thought of every one is, "When will it rain?" Prayers are offered in the churches for rain. It is also the subject of betting; and the paper this morning said that several of the prominent stockbrokers were confined to their rooms, with low spirits, on account of the condition of stocks, caused by the general depression from the dry season. We watch the sky a good deal. Strange clouds appear and disappear, but nothing comes of them. To-day, when I first looked out of my window, there were two together, before it, most human-like in appearance, that seemed to hold out their arms, as if in appeal; but, as I watched them, they only drew their beautiful trailing drapery after them, and moved slowly away.

There is a curious excitement about this weather, coming in the middle of winter. These extremes of dryness, and this strange heat at this season, reversing all natural order, may be one cause of the peculiarities of the Californians; and they are certainly peculiar people. I recently took a little excursion to Oakland, crossing the bay by the ferry, and riding some distance in the cars. A pleasant feeling came over me as I saw that it was like crossing the Merrimac from Newburyport to Salisbury; the distance was about as far, and there were the same low trees and green grass on the opposite side. I felt quite at home, until, on entering the cars, my eyes lighted on this notice, posted conspicuously everywhere: "Passengers will beware of playing three-card monte, strap, or any other game of chance, with strangers. If you do, you will surely be robbed." All visions of respectable New England vanished at that sight.

# XIV.

Quong. — His *Protégé*. — His Peace-Offering. — The Chinese and their Grandmothers. — Ancient Ideas. — Irish, French, and Spanish Chinamen. — Chinese Ingenuity. — Hostility against the Chinese. — Their Proclamations. — Discriminations against them. — Their Evasion of the Law. — Their Perseverance against all Obstacles. — Their Reverence for their Ancestors, and Fear of the Dead. — Their Medical Knowledge. — Their Belief in the Future. — Their Curious Festivals. — Indian Names for the Months. — Resemblance between the Indians and Chinese. — Their Superstitions.

San Francisco, Feb. 20, 1877.

SOME time since, we asked the washman to send us a new boy. One evening, in the midst of a great storm of wind and rain, the most grotesque little creature appeared at the door, with his bundle under his arm, as if he were sure of being accepted. We thought we must keep him for a day or two, on account of the weather, and just to show him that he could not do what we wanted; but he proved too amusing for us to think of letting him go. His name is Quong. He is shorter than Margie, who is only nine, and has much more of a baby face, but a great deal of dignity; and he assures me, when they go out together, that he shall take good care of Margie and the baby, and if there is any trouble he will call the police. We felt a little afraid to trust them with him at first, because the Chinese are so often attacked in the streets; but he has unbounded confidence in the police, and has a little whistle with which to call them. It reminds me of Robin Hood; he takes such great pleasure in making use of it, and comes out so safe from all dangers by the help of it.

The first Sunday that he was here, we told him that he could go out for a while, as all the Chinese do on that day. When he came back, I asked him where he had been. These little boy are all petted a good deal at the washhouses, and I supposed he had been there enjoying himself. But he said that he went every Sunday to see a small boy that he had charge of, who was too young to work; that he sent him now to school, but next year he should tell him, "No work, no eat;" and, if he did not do something to support himself, he should not give him clothes any more. I remember reading that the Chinese were considered men at fourteen. It is very comical to see such a little creature assume these responsibilities, and take such pride in them. He says that he is ten, but his face is perfectly infantine; and he is a baby too in his plays. He rolls and tumbles about like a young dog or kitten. If it rains, he seems like a wild duck, he is so pleased with it; and then, when the sun comes out, he hardly knows how to express his enjoyment of it; he looks at me with such a radiant face, saying, "Oh, nice sun, nice!" I feel ready at that moment to forgive him for every thing that we ever have to blame him for, — such a sun seems to shine out of him; and I feel as if we made a mistake to be critical about his little faults, which are mainly attributable to his extreme youth.

He has lately been away to celebrate the new year. "Going home to China," he calls it, because at that time the Chinese eat their national food, and observe their own customs. We told him, before he left, that he must be sure to come back in two days; but three passed, with no sign of him. Then R—— went down to the wash-house, and left word that he must come directly back. In the course of the afternoon, he walked in. The moment he opened the door, we said to him, very severely, "What for you stop too long?" But he walked up to me, without a word, and put down before me a little dirty handkerchief, all tied up in knots, which I finally made up my mind to open. It was full of the most curious sweetmeats and candy, — little curls of cocoanut, frosted with sugar; queer fruits, speckled with seeds; and some nuts that looked exactly like carved ram's-heads with horns. We had to accept this as a peace-offering, and put aside our anger.

He is much pleased to be where there is a woman. Although he is so young, he says that he has lived generally only with men, — Spanish men, he says, where there was "too much tree." I suppose it was some rather unsettled place, — a sheep-ranch, perhaps.

He is so unsophisticated that he will answer all our questions, as the older ones will not, if they can. I asked him, one day, about the ceremonies that I saw at Lone Mountain, —what they burned the red and silver paper on the graves for; and he said that in the other world the Chinamen were dressed in paper, and, if they did not burn some for them on their graves, they would not have any clothes. I told him I saw a boy kneel down on a grave, and take a cup of rice wine, and sip a little, and then pour it out on the sand. He said, Oh, no, that he did not drink any, only put it to his lips, and said, "Good-by, good-by," because the dead Chinaman would come no more.

Whenever he speaks of any thing mysterious, we can see, by the darkening of his face, how he feels the awe of it. One of his friends, in hurrying to get his ironing done, to get ready to celebrate the new year, brought on an attack of hemorrhage of the lungs. Of course, it was necessary to keep him entirely still, which his companions knew; but, at the same time, they were so afraid that he might die where he was, that they insisted on carrying him to another place, a long way off, which killed him. For, they said, if he died at the wash-house, he would come back there; and then all the Chinamen would leave, or they would have to move the house. His grandmother, the boy said, came back in a blue flame, and asked for something to eat, and they had to move the house; then she came back to where the house stood before, but could not get any farther.

The Chinese stand in great awe of their grandmothers. In their estimate of women, as in many of their other ideas, they are quite different from the rest of the world; with them a woman increases in value as she grows older. The young girl who is a slave to her mother can look forward to the prospect of being a goddess to her grandchildren.

MARCH 20, 1877.

Quong observes every thing, and asks endless questions about what he sees. He says that the French and Spanish people here like the Chinamen "too much" (a good deal); and that the "Melicans half likee, half no likee;" but the Irishmen "no likee nothing,"—seeing so plainly who their true enemies are. Many of the principal people here are Irish. On St. Patrick's Day, R—— told him that he was going to take Margie to see the procession, and that he could go too; but he said, with an air of immense superiority, that he did not care to go and see the "whiskey men;" he would rather stop at home, and do his work.

I feel now that all my responsibilities are shared. A while ago, R—— was obliged to stay out one night till twelve o'clock; and, when he came home, he found the boy, with his little black head on the kitchen table, fast asleep. When he waked him, and asked him what he was there for, he said, that, as every one else was asleep, he staid there to take care of the house. On another occasion, when R—— was to be out late again, I took pains to tell him to go right to bed, as soon as he had washed the dishes. He looked up at me, as if he were going to suggest the most insuperable obstacle to that, and asked, "Who fuff the light?" (put it out.)

One thing that I am always very much impressed with, in regard to the Chinese, is the feeling of there being something ancient about them, no matter how young they may be themselves; not only because many of them wear clothes which appear to have been handed down from their remotest ancestors, but they have ancient ideas. This boy, although he is of such a cheerful temperament, seems always to keep his own death in view, as much as the old Egyptian kings ever did. He pays a kind of burial-fee, amounting to nearly a quarter of his wages, every month, to some one appointed by the Chinese company to which he belongs; and when R—— remonstrated with him, and told him how foolish and unnecessary it was, and how much better it would be to spend the money for something else, he seemed to regard his remarks with great horror, and said he *must* pay it; to leave off wasn't to be thought of, for then, he said, he should have "no hole to get into" (meaning no grave), and there would be no apples thrown away at his funeral.

We one day heard him speaking of one of his countrymen as an Irish Chinaman; and, when we asked him what he meant, he said there were

Irish Chinamen, French Chinamen, and Spanish Chinamen. Our own observation seems to confirm this idea. We see often among them the light, careless temperament which marks the French; these are the men who support the theatres, and patronize the gaming-dens. The grave, serene Spanish is the common type; and, since the hoodlum spirit has broken out among the Californians, it has called out a coarse, rough class among the Chinese, corresponding to the lower grades of the Irish. To this class belong the "Highbinders," — men bound by secret oaths to murder, robbery, and outrage. The actual crimes that can be justly charged against the Chinese in this country are due, almost wholly, to the spirit that evoked these men.

Their ingenuity is equal to their perseverance in accomplishing an end. The Six Companies having made a regulation in regard to the washhouses, that there should be at least fifteen houses between every two of them, one of the washmen was notified that he must give up his business, there being only fourteen houses between his and the next establishment. Although the Six Companies' directions are absolute law, he had no idea of doing this. He carefully examined the fourteen buildings, and found among them a deserted pickle manufactory, which he hired for one day, with the privilege of putting up a partition which would divide it into two houses, — in that way fulfilling the requirements of the law.

April 30, 1877.

There has lately been a great excitement about the Chinese here, and several meetings have been held to consider how to get rid of them; and anti-Chinese processions, carrying banners with crossed daggers, have paraded the streets. One night the Chinese armed themselves, and went up on to the tops of their houses, prepared to fire on a mob. They issued a proclamation, saying, that they were not much accustomed to fighting (I remember learning, in the geography, that they dressed themselves in quilted petticoats when they went to battle), but they should sell their lives as dearly as they could.

Another proclamation which they sent out was very characteristic of them; it showed so good an understanding of the subject, suggesting so artfully that, if the Chinamen were not allowed unlimited freedom to come here, Americans should not be allowed to go to China.

In an "Address to the Public" which they recently put forth, they explained, that, instead of taking the places of better men, as they are accused of doing, they considered that, in performing the menial work they did, they opened the way to higher and more lucrative employments for others; saying several times, in their simple, impressive way, "We lift others up."

In regard to the other chief accusation, — that they do not profit the country any, do not invest any thing here, but send every thing home to China, — they said, "The money that you pay us for our labor, we send home; but the work remains for you," — as, for instance, the Pacific Railroad.

In trying to accumulate arguments against them, the anti-Chinese party have made a great deal of the fact that they are bound to companies, who advance money for them to come here, and say that the cooly trade is like the slave-trade. One of the anti-Chinese speakers said he helped make California a free state, and seemed to think he was employed in the same meritorious way now. Upon investigation, it proved that many of them do mortgage themselves — that is, their services — for a number of years, to get here; and that it is often in order that they may support poor relatives at home, who would otherwise starve. This shows some of their heathen virtues. A good deal of the objection to them seems to be on the ground of their being Pagans; some of the speakers saying that it is "so very demoralizing to our Christian youth," that they should be here, — quite overlooking a very large class of the population who are worse than Pagans, and vastly more dangerous.

The idea now seems to be, to drive them away by discriminating against them in State and city regulations; as, for instance, by enforcing the "pure-air ordinance," by which every Chinaman who sleeps where there is less than five hundred cubic feet of air for each person, pays a fine of ten dollars, but white people sleep as they choose. Then, as they value their cues above all things, and are greatly disgraced if they lose them, — having even been known to commit suicide when deprived of them, — an old ordinance is restored, by which every one who is put in jail must have his hair cropped close. They are often arrested on false charges. Then a special tax is levied on their wash-houses, and a new regulation made, by which no one can carry baskets on poles across the sidewalks; that being the way they carry about vegetables to sell. All these little teasing things, and a great many other annoyances which have not any pretence of legality, they bear with patience, and seem in all ways to show more forbearance even, and give, if possible, less ground for complaint, than before.

The poll-tax, which is levied on all males over twenty-one years of age, is rigorously collected from the Chinamen, while no special effort is made to collect it from the whites. In crossing the ferry to Oakland, they are often pounced upon by the collector, — in many instances when they are under age; and, unless they can show a tax receipt, their travelling bags or bundles are taken from them, and retained until the requirements of the collector are satisfied. Their wit and shrewdness avail them, however, to avoid this trouble; and a Chinaman who has occasion to cross the ferry can usually borrow the tax receipt of some one who has already paid. This serves as a passport, as it is not easy for a white man to distinguish them as individuals, on account of their similarity in dress, manners, and general appearance.

The police, being extremely vigilant in respect to all violations of law by the Chinese, have sought out their gambling-dens with great diligence, and made many arrests. The Chinese, not to be baffled, — besides resorting to labyrinthine passages, underground apartments, barricades of various kinds, and other modes of secluding themselves, to indulge in their games undisturbed, — have adopted one medium after another in place of cards, substituting something that could be quickly concealed in case the police should surprise them. At one time they made use of squash or melon seeds for this purpose, cutting on them the necessary devices. These could be much more easily concealed about the folds of their loose garments than cards. When this ruse was detected, they made use of almonds in the same way; and, when surprised, hastily devoured them, leaving not a particle of evidence upon which a policeman could base an arrest.

May 10, 1877.

One of the strongest arguments against the Chinese has been that they could never affiliate with our people, nor enter into the spirit of our institutions; that they had no desire to become citizens, and had no families here. Now that they have petitioned for common-school privileges for their children, stating how many there are here, and to what extent they are taxed to support schools, there is a louder outcry than ever against them, for such audacity. They are slowly asserting themselves, in different ways, and showing that they understand a good deal that we thought they did not. One of them has now protested against being imprisoned for violating the "pure-air ordinance." The city has made a good deal of money by the fines paid on this account, but it has been thought expedient to stop the arrests while this case is being tried.

Then they are making an effort against the injustice of the city in discriminating against them by charging more for laundry licenses where the clothes are carried about by hand, than where horses are used; in this way obliging any one who does a small business to pay more in proportion than one who does a large business. There are a great many large French laundries here, that all send about wagons. The Chinese carry every thing by hand; they seem altogether too meek and timid to have horses; but, as they adapt themselves to every thing, they have looked about, and met the difficulty, in part, by securing quite a number of poor, abject animals, with which they are beginning to appear in the streets. There is no change they are not willing to make; and their patience and perseverance are unconquerable, about staying and going on with their work. As an Eastern writer said of them: "They bow to the storm, and rise up, and plod on in the intervals." It is very true of them, as we see them here, — so unresisting, and yet so resistless.

We have lately made the acquaintance of a man who has lived thirty years in Shanghae, who explained many of their customs and ideas. He confirmed some things that our boys had told us, but we understood them better from him. He said that the Chinese have such perfect faith in continued life after death, and in a man's increased power in another life, that it was not an unusual thing for any one who had some great injury to avenge, to kill himself, in order to get into a position to do it more effectually. To them a dead man is more important than a living one; and the one great feature of their religion is the worship of their ancestors. They make a great many offerings to them, — as we saw them do at Lone Mountain. If any one dies at sea, or in a foreign country, where there is no friend or relative to do this for him, he becomes a beggar spirit. It is the duty of the Chinese at home to make offerings to beggar spirits as well as to their own relatives. If any great misfortune happens to a man, he thinks he must have neglected or offended some dead relative, or perhaps one of these beggar spirits; and will impoverish himself for years, to atone for it by a great feast. They are very much afraid of the spirits, and build their houses with intricate passages, and put up screens, to keep them from seeing what happens; and they especially avoid openings north and south, as they think the spirits move only in north and south lines. What is more important than almost any thing in a man's life, is to be placed right after his death, — toward the south, that he may receive genial and reviving influences from it; but if he is toward the north, and gets chilling influences from that direction, he wreaks his vengeance on his living relatives who placed him there.

We learn a good deal from the boys we have. I should like very much to go into their schools, they are so well taught in many respects. One of our boys once took some fruit-wax, and modelled a perfect little duck. He said he was taught at school how to do it. He also drew several animals with an exceedingly life-like appearance. This early instruction is no doubt the basis of the acknowledged superiority of the Chinese as carvers in wood and ivory.

I have often wondered that more of them do not die in coming to a climate so different from their own, and adopting such new modes of life as most of them are obliged to do. But they all seem to have been taught the rudiments of medicine. A young American boy, if he is sick, has not the remotest idea what to do for himself; but the Chinese boys know in most cases. We have often seen them steeping their little tin cups of seeds, roots, or leaves on the kitchen stove, which they said was medicine for some ailment or other, but "Melican man no sabbe Chinaman medicine;" and sometimes, when they did not have their own remedies at hand, I have offered them pellets or tinctures from my homœopathic supply, which they could rarely be induced to accept, alleging that "Melican medicine no good for Chinaman." One of our little boys went to a Chinese doctor for himself one day, and when he came back, I asked him what the doctor said. He told me that he pressed with his finger here and there on his flesh, to see if it rose readily, and the color came back. I saw that he meant if any one was not very sick, that the flesh was elastic; and I thought it was quite a good test, and one that might perhaps be useful to our doctors. They have one curious idea in their treatment, which is, that, if any one is sick, he is to eat an additional meal instead of less. Nevertheless, they seem to get well with this arrangement.

The belief in a future life, and in improved conditions hereafter, seems to be universal among them. A poor Chinaman was found dead near us, with a letter beside him, which was translated at the inquest held over the body.

THIRD MONTH, 27th DAY [May 4].

TO MY FATHER AND MOTHER, — I came to this country, and spent my money at the gambling-table, and have not accomplished any thing. Where I am now, I cannot raise money to return home. I am sick, and have not long to live. My life has been a useless one. When you have read this letter, do not cry yourselves sick on my account. Let my brothers' wives rear and educate my two cousins. I wish to be known as godfather to one of them. I desire Chow He, my wife, to protect and assist you. When you both are dead, she may marry if she wishes. In this world I can do no more for you, father and mother. You must look to the next world for any future benefit to be received from me.

TONG GOOT LOON.

SEPT. 10, 1877.

The Chinese generally appear unwilling to talk with us about their religious customs and ideas, apparently from superstitious feelings. Occasionally we meet with an intelligent one, who readily answers our questions, and tells us about many of their festivals celebrated at home, which are not recognized here. Notwithstanding their solemn faces and methodical ways, they are as fond of celebrations as the San Francisco people themselves. They celebrate the Festival of the Little Cold, and of the Great Cold; of the Little Snow, and of the Great Snow; of the Moderate Heat, and of the Great Heat. Early in the autumn comes the Festival of Pak-lo, or the White Dew; later in the autumn, the Festival of Hon-lo, or the Cold Dew. About the time of our harvest moon, the fifteenth day of eighth moon, they celebrate the Festival of the Full Moon, eating moon-cakes, and sending presents to their friends, of tea, wine, and fruits; in February, the Festival of Rain and Water; early in the spring (the sixth day of second moon), the Festival of Enlivened Insects. On the third day of third moon they celebrate, for three days and nights, the birthday of Pak Tai, god of the extreme north; in spring, the birthday of the god of health; in spring also, the great Festival of Tsing Ming (Clear and Bright). On this occasion, they visit and worship at the tombs. In all great festivals the ancestors must share. In early summer occurs the Festival of the Prematurely Ripened. The hour for the offering of each sacrifice is most carefully chosen, — that of the spring sacrifice being at the first glimmering of dawn.

This shows as close observation of nature on their part as the Indians display, and reminds me of the names the Makahs give to the months: December, the moon when the gray whale appears; March, the moon of the fin-back whale; April, the moon of sprouts and buds; May, the moon of the salmon-berry; June, the moon of the red huckleberry; November, the moon of winds and screaming birds. The Makahs select the time of the full moon as an especially favorable one to communicate with the Great Spirit.

I do not know whether it is now considered that our Indians are of Oriental origin. It seems at first as if two races could hardly differ more than Indians and Chinese; but, after living long among them, many resemblances attract our attention. We have seen, occasionally, Indians with quite Mongolian features, and short, square frames. Flattening the head among the Indians is considered a mark of distinction, as compressing the feet is with the Chinese; no slave being allowed to practise either. The reverence of the Indians for the graves of their fathers approaches the worship of ancestors among the Chinese. No outrage is greater to the Indians than to desecrate the burial-places of their dead. They often make sacrifices to them, and celebrate anniversaries of the dead with dancing and feasting. The Chinese feast their dead at regular intervals, and carry them thousands of miles across the ocean from foreign countries to rest in their own land at last. The Manitous (ruling spirits) of earth, air, and water, with the Indians, are, in some respects, like the Shin of the Chinese, — spirits that inhabit all nature; but the Shin are inferior deities, not having much power, being employed rather as detectives, — as the kitchen god, or hearth spirit, who at the end of the year reports the conduct of the family to Shang-te, the God of Heaven. Both races are firm believers in the power and efficacy of charms: the Chinaman, in his green-jade bracelet, is demon-proof; the Indian warrior, in a white wolf-skin, rides to certain victory. Both are excessively superstitious, considering that the ruling spirits are sometimes friendly, sometimes hostile; and feel it necessary, in all the commonest acts of their lives, to be constantly on the watch to guard against malign influences, — attributing great power for harm to the spirits of the dead. An Indian, like a Chinaman, will frequently abandon his lodge, thinking some dead relative whom he has offended has discovered him there. He is afraid to speak the name of any one who is dead, and often changes his own name, that the dead person, not hearing the old name spoken, may not so readily find him. Indians and Chinese are alike in the habit of changing their names, having one for youth, another for manhood, and a third for old age; taking new names many times in the course of their lives, — as after any great event or performance.

They resemble each other in their infatuation for gambling, — a Chinaman, after all his possessions have been staked and lost, sometimes selling himself for a term of years, to keep up the game; or an Indian gambling away a hand, an arm, a leg, and so on, and at last the head, until the whole body is lost at the play, and then he goes into perpetual slavery. The Indians will sometimes gamble away their children, though they are usually very fond of them, — the typical "bad Indian" with them being one who is cowardly, or who neglects his children.

## XV.

**Chun Fa's Funeral. — Alameda. — Gophers and Lizards. — Poison Oak. — Sturdy Trees. — Baby Lizards. — Old Alameda. — Emperor Norton. — California Generosity. — The Dead Newsboy. — Anniversary of the Goddess Kum Fa. — Chinese Regard for the Moon and Flowers. — A Shin Worshipper.**

**ALAMEDA, CAL., April 5, 1878.**

WE have left San Francisco, and come across the bay to live. The last thing I did there was to go to a Chinawoman's funeral. I saw in the papers that Chun Fa, the wife of Loy Mong, was dead; and he would like to have all the Christian Chinese and their friends come to the funeral. I thought I would go. Especially at this time, when the Chinese meet with so much bad treatment, we are glad of an opportunity to show our good-will and sympathy; but I did not expect to be so much interested as I was. The columns in the chapel were wreathed with ivy and lilies, and every thing was very quiet and pleasant in the bright forenoon. One side of the church was filled with Chinese women and girls. It is very hard to tell which are women, and which are children, they all have such childlike faces. I suppose it is because they are so undeveloped. Their uncovered heads, and smooth, shining black hair, looked to me at first all exactly alike; all the company seemed of one pattern. But, when I had noticed them longer, I saw some variety in their manners and expressions. To sit there among them, and feel the differences between them and us, and the resemblances, — so much stronger than the differences, — was a curious experience.

It was a school, I found, and Chun Fa seemed to have been the flower of it. They all mourned very much at losing her. She was the wife of one of their principal merchants, — but their wives are often children. She had a sweet, innocent face; and we heard that she was very intelligent, and eager to learn. With her fair, open look, it seemed as if one could have done a great deal with her in the way of development.

An American man first made a prayer in Chinese; then they all sang —

"Shall we gather at the river?"

in English. They sang with so much fervor,

that, although it was so unmusical, I felt more like crying than laughing, to think it was for one of those Chinese women who have been so badly spoken of; the papers often saying that they are all prostitutes, that there are no families among them, and that the California people must purify their State by getting rid of them. Then a serene-looking Chinaman chanted something that sounded very soothing and musical, and another made a prayer. Then we went, each one, and took leave of poor little Chun Fa. I thought I should have been willing to have it my funeral, every thing was so genuine about it; no cant, and nothing superfluous.

We met with quite a disappointment in leaving San Francisco, to find that our little Quong could not go with us. We thought we had obtained leave from the proper patron; but at the last a brother appeared who claimed to be superior authority, and forbade his going. As he seemed a very gruff, disagreeable person, and, as the boy said, had never treated him kindly, we advised him to disobey him; but he said it would never do for a little China boy to disobey a father or an older brother; but, when he was old enough, he would take ten dollars, and buy a pistol, and shoot him.

April 30, 1878.

We are only an hour's ride by cars and steamer from San Francisco. It is hard to believe it, it is so wholly different a place. Before us is a field of blue nemophilas. To see them waving in the wind, recalled to me what Emerson said about its restoring any one to reason and faith to live in the midst of nature, — so many trivial cares and anxieties disappeared at the sight of it. On the other side, the water rolls softly up to our very door. We bathe in it, floating about at will in warm or cold currents.

The first morning after we moved here, I noticed two small hills and holes, newly dug, beside our door. A curious little head thrust itself out of one, and two small eyes peered at me. They belonged to one of the little underground creatures, called gophers, that we have all about us. They eat roots, and it is almost impossible to cultivate any thing where they are. They appeared to have come just because they saw that the house was going to be occupied. I think they like human company, only they want to keep their own distance. They and the lizards quite animate the landscape. The gopher's wise, old-fashioned looking head is quite a contrast to that of the lizard, with its eager, inquisitive expression. There is always a little twisted-up head and bright eye, or a sharp little tail, appearing and disappearing, wherever we look. They spend their whole time in coming and going. Their purpose seems to be accomplished, if they succeed in seeing us, and getting safely away.

The wagoner who moved us over from San Francisco made some commiserating remarks concerning me, as he deposited the last load of furniture; saying that it was a good place to raise children, but would be very solitary for the woman.

It is a lonely place here, but the water is constant company. As I write, the only sound I can hear is the gentle roll of waves, and now and then an under sound that seems to come from far-off caverns, — so soft and so deep. I never lived so close to the water before, so that its changes made a part of my every-day life. Even when I am so busy that I do not look at it, I feel how the tide is creeping in, filling up all the little inlets, and making all waste places bright and full.

MAY 10, 1878.

We made inquiries of some of the old residents, in reference to the wind, before we decided to come here; but people who live in half-settled places, I find, are very apt to misrepresent, — they are so eager for neighbors. How much wiser we should have been to have consulted the trees! — they show so plainly that they have fought all their lives against a strong sea-wind, bending low, and twisting themselves about, trying to get away from it.

We find that where we live is not Alameda proper, but is called the Encinal District, — *encinal* being the Spanish for *oak*. I do not know whether they mean by it the old dusky evergreens, or the poison oak which is every where their inseparable companion. Soon after we arrived, we found ourselves severely affected by it. It was then in flower, and we attributed its strength to that circumstance; but every change it passes through re-enforces its life, — when it ripens its berries, when its leaves turn bright, or when the autumn rains begin. Every thing suits it; moisture or dryness, whichever prevails, appears to be its element. Thoreau, who liked to see weeds overrun flowers, would have rejoiced in its vigor. We never touch it; but any one sensitive to its influence cannot pass near it, nor breathe the air where it grows, without being affected by it. Alameda seems hardly ready for human occupancy yet, unless something effectual can be done to exterminate it. We often see superficial means taken, like burning it down to the level of the earth; but what short-sighted warfare is that which gives new strength after a brief interval! On one account I forgive it many injuries, — that it furnishes our only bright autumn foliage, turning into most vivid and beautiful shades of red. Except for the poison oak, and a few of the long, narrow leaves of the Eucalyptus, that hang like party-colored ribbons on the trees, we have no change in the foliage between summer and winter; there are always the same old dingy evergreen oaks everywhere about us.

There are some cultivated grounds and gardens in the neighborhood, but everywhere interspersed among them are wild fields. The trees have a determined look, as they stand and hold possession of them. The cultivated ones that border the streets, in contrast with them, appear quite tame. I find myself thinking of the latter sometimes as if they were artificial, and only these old aborigines were real; they have so much more character and expression. I heard a lady criticising Alameda, saying that there were so many trees, you could not see the place. We have a general feeling, all the time, as if we were camping out, and everybody else were camping out too. The trees are scattered everywhere; and it is quite the fashion, in this humble part of the town, for people to live in tents while they build their own houses. These trees are of a very social kind, bending low, and spreading their branches wide, so that any one could almost live in them just as they are. They are a great contrast to the firs which we had wholly around us on Puget Sound. They have strange fancies for twisting and turning. I have never seen two alike, nor one that grew up straight. It is not because they are so yielding, — they are as stiff and rugged as they can be, — it must be their own wild nature that makes them like to grow in strange, irregular ways. Sometimes, when I look at great fields of them, I feel as if I were in the midst of a storm, every thing has such a wind-swept look, although it is perfectly still at the time. One day I came upon a body of them, that appeared as if they had all been stopped by some sudden enchantment, in the midst of running away. Often we see trees that look as if they had come out of the wars, with great clefts in their sides, and holes through them. Their foliage is very slight; there is very little to conceal their muscular look. It seems as if we could feel in them the will that tightened all the fibres.

MAY 15, 1878.

The great event to us lately has been the advent of the baby lizards. The streets are all laid with planks, clean and sunny. The lizards delight in them, they are so bright and warm. I like to see, as I walk along, these curious little bodies, in old-fashioned scale armor, stopping and looking about, as if they were drinking in the comfort of the sunshine, just as I am. Although they stop a great deal, it is very difficult to catch one, for their movements are like a flash. I did succeed once in holding one long enough to examine his beautiful steel-blue bands. The babies are as delicate as if they were made of glass, and as light and airy as if they belonged to fairy-land. They run, all the time, backward and forward, just for the pleasure of moving, over the sidewalk, and under it.

When I read in the papers, every week, about the people who kill themselves in San Francisco, — and they generally say that they do it because there does not seem to be any thing worth living for, — I wonder if it would not make a difference to them if they lived in the country, and saw how entertaining the world looks to the lively little creatures about us, who think it worth while to move so quickly, and look well about on every side, for fear they may miss seeing something.

JULY 2, 1878.

When we first came here in the spring, and found the ground all blue and yellow and white with blossoms, I thought how interested I should be, to watch the succession of flowers. But that was all. In these dry places, we have only *spring* flowers. I did, though, the other day, see something red in the distance, and, going to it, found a clump of thistles, almost as tall as I am, of a bright crimson color. The fields are very dry now, and it seems to be the season of the snakes. Under the serpent-like branches, we find nothing but the cast-off skins of the snakes.

There are some curious old men here who tend cattle, sitting under the trees, with their knitting. I think they are Germans. They do not appear to understand when I speak to them. I thought they might be "broke miners," who are generally the most curious people hereabouts.

One of these" broke miners " is employed to take care of two little children near us, whose mother is dead. He dresses them with their clothes hind-side before, and liable at any moment to drop entirely off; but seems to succeed very well in amusing them, quilting up his dish-cloths into dolls for them, and transforming their garments into kites. His failing seems to be that a kind of dreamy mood is apt to steal over him, in which he wanders on the beach, regardless of hours; and the master of the house, coming home, has to hunt high and low for him, to come and prepare the meal. On the last bright moonlight night, he wholly disappeared.

OCT. 15, 1878.

We have finally been driven off by the wind from our cottage on the bay. Margie has been so accustomed to moving, that she takes it as easily as an Indian child would. A few days before we left, she gave me an account of the moving of the man opposite, which was all accomplished before breakfast in the morning. First, she said, he put all his things on a wagon, and then took his house to pieces, and put that on; and then he and the wagoner sat down and drank a pot of coffee together, and started off, on their load.

We did not take our house with us, but found a rather dilapidated one, in what is called Old Alameda. It is quite attractive, from the trees and vines about it, and the spacious garden in which it stands. It is owned by an old German woman, who lives next to us. She is rich now, and owns the whole block, but still holds to her old peasant customs, and wears wooden shoes. Opposite is a French family, who go off every year to a vineyard, to make wine; and, next to them, a poor Spanish family, who carry round mussels to sell.

MARCH 3, 1879.

We have had a real winter; not that it was very cold or snowy, — that it never is here, — but so excessively rainy as to keep us a good deal in-doors. The grass grew up in the house, and waved luxuriantly round the edges of the rooms. The oak-trees surprised us by bursting out into fresh young green, though we had not noticed that they had lost any of their hard, evergreen leaves.

APRIL 10, 1879.

While we were crossing the ferry between San Francisco and Oakland one day, a peculiar-looking person appeared on the deck of the boat, who saluted the assembled company in a most impressive manner. He was a large man, serene and self-possessed, with rather a handsome face. On his broad shoulders he wore massive epaulets, a sword hung by his side, and his hat was crowned with nodding peacock feathers. I noticed that he passed the gates where the tickets are delivered, unquestioned, giving only a courteous salute, instead of the customary passport. Upon inquiry, I learned that he was the "Emperor Norton, ruler of California," according to his fancy; and that he passed free wherever he chose to go, — theatres opening their doors to him, railroads and steamers conveying him without charge. He was an old pioneer, distraught by misfortunes, and humored in this hallucination by the people. He was in the habit of ordering daily telegraphic despatches sent to the different crowned heads of Europe. He had once been known to draw his sword upon his washer-woman, because she presumed to demand payment for his washing; whereupon the Pioneer Society, learning of the affair, took upon itself the charge of meeting all little expenses of this nature.

The Californians have a jolly, good-natured way of regarding idiosyncrasies, and a kind of lavish generosity in the distribution of their alms, quite different from the careful and judicious method of the Eastern people. We hear that some of the early miners, passing along the streets of San Francisco, just after it had been devastated by one of the terrible fires that swept every thing before them, and seeing a lone woman sitting and weeping among the ruins, flung twenty-dollar gold pieces and little packages of gold dust at her, until all her losses were made good, and she had a handsome overplus to start anew.

I noticed in Oakland a man who drew the whole length of his body along the sidewalk, like an enormous reptile, moving slowly by the the help of his hands, unable to get along in any other way, holding up a bright, sunny, sailor face. On his back was a pack of newspapers, from which men helped themselves, and flung him generally a half or a quarter of a dollar, always refusing the change. That such a man could do business in the streets, was a credit to the kindliness of the people incommoded by him. I hardly think he would have been tolerated in New York or Boston; but his pleasant face and fast-disappearing papers showed that he was not made uncomfortably aware of the inconvenience he caused.

One day, while waiting at the ferry, I saw two men employed in a way that attracted the attention of every one who passed. One of them, who had in his hand a pair of crutches, ascended some steps, and, crossing them, nailed them to the wall, close to the gateway where the passengers passed to the boat. The other arranged some light drapery in the form of wings above them. Below they put a small table, with the photograph of a little newsboy on it. All the business-men, the every-day passengers crossing to their homes on the Oakland side, appeared to understand it, and quietly laid some piece of money beside the picture. It seems that it was the stand of a little crippled boy who had for a year or two furnished the daily papers to the passengers passing to the boat. The money was for his funeral expenses, and to help his family. It was very characteristic of the Californians to take this dramatic and effective way of collecting a fund. Men who would have been very likely to meet a subscription-paper with indifference, on being appealed to in this poetic manner, with no word spoken, only seeing the discarded crutches and the white wings above, with moist eyes laid their little tribute below, as if it were a satisfaction to do so. I thought how the little newsboy's face would have brightened if he could have seen it, and hoped that he might not be beyond all knowledge of it now.

We have had an opportunity to observe some fine-looking Chinamen who have been at work on the railroad all winter opposite our house. There are a hundred or more of them. We understand that they are from the rural districts of China. They are large, strong, and healthy, quite different from the miserable, stunted, sallow-faced creatures from the cities, of whom we see so many, showing that this inferiority is not inherent in the race, but is the effect of unfavorable circumstances.

May 15, 1879.

Day before yesterday was the anniversary of the birthday of the Chinese goddess Kum Fa, or Golden Flower, guardian of children. She is worshipped chiefly by women; but some of the workers on the railroad begged branches of the feathery yellow acacia, which is now in bloom, to carry with them to the temple in San Francisco. They are so unpoetic in many ways, that we should hardly expect them to be so fond of flowers; but they mourn very much if the bulbs which they keep growing in stones and water in their houses in the winter do not open for the new year.

The moon and the flowers they enjoy more than any thing else. In many things they are children, and like what children like. The moon holds a very important place to them, and the dates of the new year and all their festivals are determined by its changes. We used to see one of our boys standing, sometimes for hours together, with his arms folded, gazing into the moonlit sky. When questioned as to what he was doing, he said he was "looking at the garden in the moon," and listening to "hear the star-men sing."

This boy appeared to be a Shin worshipper. He made many drawings representing these spirits, with astonishing facility and artistic skill, but, when pressed to explain them, said it was not good to speak much about them. Some rode upon clouds; some thrust their heads out of the water, or danced upon the backs of fishes; some looked out of caves among the hills. There were serene, peaceful ones, with flowers or musical instruments in their hands; others were fierce and hostile, brandishing weapons, and exploding bombs. Everywhere was the wildest freedom and grace, and apparently much symbolic meaning which we could not understand.

# LEE AND SHEPARD'S NEW BOOKS.

## *LIFE AT PUGET SOUND*

### WITH SKETCHES OF TRAVEL IN

### WASHINGTON TERRITORY, BRITISH COLUMBIA, OREGON, AND CALIFORNIA. 1865 - 1881.

BY

### CAROLINE C. LEIGHTON.

The vast inland sea, popularly known as Puget Sound, ramifying in various directions, the wide-spreading and majestic forests, the ranges of snow-capped mountains on either side, the mild and equable climate, and the diversified resources of this fav red region, ex ite the astonishment and admiration of all beholders. To the lovers of the grand and beautiful, unmarred as yet by any human interference, and untrammelled by the conventionalities which pertain to longer settled portions of the globe, it presents an endless field for observation and enjoyment. There is already a steady stream of emigration to this new "land of promise," and everything seems to indicate for it a vigorous growth and development, and a brilliant and substantial future.

---

## THE GOLDEN TRUTH SERIES.

A uniform edition of unequalled selections from the best religious authors. Edited by Mrs C. A. Means. Dainty volumes, in gold and colors, each, $1.25. Comprising: —

### GOLDEN TRUTHS.

"Abounds in gems of truth and beautiful suggestions. A book from which the thoughtful will gather hope."—*Baltimore American.*

### LIVING THOUGHTS.

"A sweet volume of selections from the best writers for Christian instruction, meditation, and comfort."—*Christian Secretary, Hartford.*

### WORDS OF HOPE.

"A volume of religious selections designed for the cheer and consolation of sorrowing friends. Sympathy for a friend in sorrow can be expressed in no more delicate or acceptable manner than by the presentation of these words of hope."—*Boston Post.*

---

## EUROPEAN BREEZES.

By Margery Deane. Cloth, gilt top, $1 50. Being chapters of travel through Germany, Austria, Hungary, and Switzerland.

"It is just the story that a bright, intelligent woman could relate to a circle of friends, and is written in a snappy, off-hand style. The travels of the writer were mostly confined to the German countries of Europe and to an incursion into that little-travelled country of Hungary. The last chapter in the book is in some respects the best, for it is the most practical, giving, as it does, information in regard to the expenses of a European trip that many an extended traveller has searched for long and f r, in vain." — *Oregonian.*

Sold by all booksellers, or sent by mail, post-paid, on receipt of price.

LEE AND SHEPARD, Publishers,

Boston, Mass.

# LEE AND SHEPARD'S NEW BOOKS.

## WHAT SHALL WE DO WITH OUR DAUGHTERS?

Superfluous Women and other Lectures. By Mrs. Mary A. Livermore. Price, $1.25.

"Earnest, sensible, and elevating in tone, these discourses express with sincerity and power the best thoughts of the day regarding the momentous topics with which they deal, and will long be a beacon light to guide the aspirations of the future."—*Boston Traveller.*

"Mrs. Livermore's book is something to be glad of, and will always have an historic interest as marking the evolution of an existing social question."—*Boston Transcript.*

## TWELVE MONTHS IN AN ENGLISH PRISON.

By Mrs. S. B. Fletcher. 12mo. Cloth. $1.50.

*** This volume contains a most thrilling narrative of the experiences of a well-known spiritualist in a situation where the visible ministrations of invisible forces are proven by the testimony of the jailers themselves. Its appearance is destined to create a profound impression, and probably a most lively discussion.

"Many of the scenes and incidents are startling, and if the book should fail to change certain notions in regard to spiritualism, it certainly will confound sceptical thinkers and writers."—*Boston Transcript.*

## HIS TRIUMPH.

By Mrs. Mary A. Denison. Author of "That Husband of Mine," "Like a Gentleman," etc. 16mo. Cloth. $1.00.

"This brightly told domestic idyl deals with actors and theatrical affairs, in the midst of which personages and scenes, the heroine, a charming young wife, acts out a little comedy of her own. This sprightly account of how a modern Eve circumvented a nineteenth-century serpent is sure to find favor with novel readers."—*The Art Interchange.*

**Uniform with Lee and Shepard's Dollar Novels.**

| | |
|---|---|
| LIKE A GENTLEMAN. | THE PUDDLEFORD PAPER. |
| NUMA ROUMESTAN. | THE FORTUNATE ISLAND. |
| KINGS IN EXILE. | THE TIGHT SQUEEZE. |

## FORE AND AFT.

A Personal Narrative of Sea Experiences. By Robert B. Dixon. 16mo. Cloth. 320 pages. Price, $1.25.

This is a book which, like the famous "Two Years Before the Mast," interests young and old alike, and is decidedly pleasant reading to a sea-lover. It has the air of VRAISEMBLANCE, and holds one with the fascination of real struggles with storms and fire and mutiny, and all the perils and marvels of the ever-changing sea.

Sold by all Booksellers, and sent by mail, post-paid, on receipt of price.

**LEE AND SHEPARD, Publishers,**

**BOSTON.**

www.ingramcontent.com/pod-product-compliance
Lightning Source LLC
Chambersburg PA
CBHW031944230426
43672CB00010B/2048

* 9 7 8 3 3 3 7 2 0 5 9 0 4 *